Implementing Outcomes Assessment: Promise and Perils

Trudy W. Banta, *Editor*
University of Tennessee, Knoxville

NEW DIRECTIONS FOR INSTITUTIONAL RESEARCH
PATRICK T. TERENZINI, *Editor-in-Chief*
University of Georgia
MARVIN W. PETERSON, *Associate Editor*
University of Michigan

Number 59, Fall 1988

Paperback sourcebooks in
The Jossey-Bass Higher Education Series

Jossey-Bass Inc., Publishers
San Francisco • London

Trudy W. Banta (ed.).
Implementing Outcomes Assessment: Promise and Perils.
New Directions for Institutional Research, no. 59.
Volume XV, Number 3.
San Francisco: Jossey-Bass, 1988.

New Directions for Institutional Research
Patrick T. Terenzini, *Editor-in-Chief*
Marvin W. Peterson, *Associate Editor*

New Directions for Institutional Research is published quarterly by
Jossey-Bass Inc., Publishers (publication number USPS 098-830), and
is sponsored by the Association for Institutional Research. The
volume and issue numbers above are included for the convenience of
libraries. Second-class postage paid at San Francisco, California, and at
additional mailing offices. POSTMASTER: Send address changes
to Jossey-Bass Inc., Publishers, 350 Sansome Street, San Francisco,
California 94104.

Editorial correspondence should be sent to the Editor-in-Chief,
Patrick T. Terenzini, Institute of Higher Education, University of
Georgia, Athens, Georgia 30602.

Library of Congress Catalog Card Number LC 85-645339

International Standard Serial Number ISSN 0271-0579

International Standard Book Number ISBN 1-55542-888-6

Cover art by WILLI BAUM

Manufactured in the United States of America. Printed on acid-free paper.

Ordering Information

The paperback sourcebooks listed below are published quarterly and can be ordered either by subscription or single copy.

Subscriptions cost $48.00 per year for institutions, agencies, and libraries. Individuals can subscribe at the special rate of $36.00 per year *if payment is by personal check.* (Note that the full rate of $48.00 applies if payment is by institutional check, even if the subscription is designated for an individual.) Standing orders are accepted.

Single copies are available at $11.95 when payment accompanies order. (California, New Jersey, New York, and Washington, D.C., residents please include appropriate sales tax.) For billed orders, cost per copy is $11.95 plus postage and handling.

Substantial discounts are offered to organizations and individuals wishing to purchase bulk quantities of Jossey-Bass sourcebooks. Please inquire.

Please note that these prices are for the calendar year 1988 and are subject to change without notice. Also, some titles may be out of print and therefore not available for sale.

To ensure correct and prompt delivery, all orders must give either the *name of an individual* or an *official purchase order number.* Please submit your order as follows:

Subscriptions: specify series and year subscription is to begin.
Single Copies: specify sourcebook code (such as, IR1) and first two words of title.

Mail orders for United States and Possessions, Latin America, Canada, Japan, Australia, and New Zealand to:
    Jossey-Bass Inc., Publishers
    350 Sansome Street
    San Francisco, California 94104

Mail orders for all other parts of the world to:
    Jossey-Bass Limited
    28 Banner Street
    London EC1Y 8QE

New Directions for Institutional Research Series
Patrick T. Terenzini *Editor-in-Chief*
Marvin W. Peterson, *Associate Editor*

Contents

Editor's Notes

The 1980s might be called the age of assessment in higher education. State interest in having institutions demonstrate the quality of the education provided with public dollars was first manifested in the performance-funding initiative of the Tennessee Higher Education Commission in 1979. In 1984, coordinating agencies in New Jersey and Virginia provided incentive grants to lead institutions to design their own outcomes assessment programs. Between the highly structured Tennessee model and the relatively unstructured approaches used in New Jersey and Virginia lies a variety of other recent state initiatives to encourage colleges and universities to undertake assessment. By 1987, a study conducted for the Education Commission of the States had revealed that two-thirds of the states had taken steps to acquire evidence of public institutions' accountability for producing desired outcomes for students (Boyer, Ewell, Finney, and Mingle, 1987).

A half-dozen national reports between 1984 and 1987, including the NIE Study Group's (1984) *Involvement in Learning* and Boyer's (1987) *College: The Undergraduate Experience in America*, have called attention to the need for evaluation and responsive improvements in higher education. Private colleges and universities have begun to feel the pressure to undertake assessment programs: Each of the six regional accrediting associations has adopted a standard similar to the Southern Association of Colleges and Schools' "institutional effectiveness" criterion. According to El-Khawas (1987), faculty and administrators on three-fourths of the nation's campuses were discussing assessment in the spring of 1987. Of this group, half were developing assessment procedures and 80 percent expected to introduce some form of assessment in the next few years.

It will come as no surprise to institutional researchers that most institutions have recognized the need to look carefully at ways of evaluating program effectiveness, and that many are taking steps to develop comprehensive assessment programs. As the primary source of information about the institution and its students, the office of institutional research must be a key participant in any campuswide assessment program.

Despite all the interest in assessment and the pressure to accomplish it, it is difficult to define assessment precisely. For the purposes of this volume, *outcomes assessment* means collecting evidence of (1) student performance on specified measures of development, (2) program strengths and weaknesses, and (3) institutional effectiveness. By looking at what students and graduates know and are able to do with their knowledge, as

1

well as at their perceptions of the quality of institutional programs and services, researchers can obtain important information about programs' ability to meet stated objectives for student development. The collective quality of its programs establishes the effectiveness of an institution.

Responsibility for planning a campus assessment program is usually assigned to a representative group of key administrators and faculty leaders. The group may meet for months, even for years, before making recommendations, because reviews of literature and of available instruments raise many more questions than they answer. For example, if one standardized exam in a field does not match curricular objectives very well, is it better to use it anyway, since it does at least provide external norms, or should a new exam be developed? Another issue concerns how to motivate students to do their best work on a chosen test.

The assessment planning committee usually is not granted the luxury of sufficient time to resolve all its questions and concerns. Pressure from campus administrators, state lawmakers, regional accreditors, and others is too great to permit long delays in beginning to collect some kind of data on program effectiveness; delays may be viewed as foot-dragging tactics by anyone not privy to the planning committee's deliberations.

Most of us who write about assessment believe that institutions can derive substantial benefits from comprehensive assessment programs. To date, we have focused our energies on writing positive articles designed to help campus representatives find answers to their questions about techniques and procedures. Peter Ewell's (1985) volume of New Directions for Institutional Research contained three institutional case studies and three chapters on specific assessment methods. The title of Diane Halpern's (1987) more recent sourcebook, *Student Outcomes Assessment: What Institutions Stand to Gain,* leaves no doubt that the position papers and reports on institutional experiences have certainly contributed to the case for assessment. Institutional researchers and others trained in the methodology of educational research and measurement have known from the outset, however, that demonstrating quality through outcomes assessment would be fraught with pitfalls. Doing creditable assessment is tough work. Because of the pressure to get started, to measure something, we have used some instruments that were readily available, even though less than 50 percent of the content actually matched what we were teaching our students. In other instances, we have developed our own tests by using items from files of departmental classroom tests, without regard for item clarity or reliability. In the early history of outcomes assessment in higher education, we have used ad hoc procedures and invalid instruments because we have not had the time to seek a strong theoretical base for our work. This was certainly not the first time that practitioners had plunged ahead of theoreticians, but now it is time to take stock of where we have been, what we have accomplished, and where we should go next in strengthening our approaches to assessment.

Several of the authors who contributed to this volume have written previously about the promise of assessment. We have not lost sight of that feature, but here optimism is tempered by realism. Along with its promise, some of the perils of assessment are identified and discussed.

The chapters in this sourcebook present a general overview followed by exploration of several specific issues and then by a case study. Richard I. Miller (Chapter One) and Peter T. Ewell (Chapter Two) provide the overview. Miller believes that the current interest in institutionalizing outcomes assessment could be served by a thorough study of how organizational change is implemented. Ewell focuses on administrative concerns related to implementing assessment and provides pragmatic suggestions on discovering purposes for assessment, converting data to information, and promoting the use of assessment information by campus decision makers.

Specific issues in the implementation of outcomes assessment are addressed in Chapters Three through Six by Jonathan Warren, Oscar T. Lenning, Gary R. Hanson, and Darrell R. Lewis. Warren and Lenning give examples of instruments and procedures that faculty and administrators can use to gather information about cognitive and noncognitive student outcomes. In Chapter Five, Hanson explores a key assessment issue—the feasibility of calculating gain scores, or value added, when students' behavior is measured on two or more occasions. In Chapter Six, Lewis proposes a typology of costs and benefits associated with assessment, and he recommends that both be weighed carefully before a decision is made to invest in assessment as a means of acquiring information.

Chapter Seven, by Trudy W. Banta, contains a case study of the development and evolution of Tennessee's strategy for encouraging institutions in that state to engage in outcomes assessment. Tennessee's pioneering performance-funding policy has survived one five-year cycle and been renewed for another, with increased emphasis on levels of test scores and other quantifiable data.

Chapter Eight, also by Banta, presents a summary of the assets and liabilities of assessment, as identified by the authors of the foregoing chapters. Suggestions are given for minimizing the perils and maximizing the promise of assessment in higher education. Chapter Nine, by Gary R. Pike, lists centers and institutions that can be consulted for more information about the implementation of assessment. The chapter also includes an annotated bibliography of key references in this young but growing field.

Trudy W. Banta
Editor

4

References

Boyer, C. M., Ewell, P. T., Finney, J. E., and Mingle, J. R. "Assessment and Out-comes Measurement: A View from the States." *AAHE Bulletin,* 1987, *39* (7), 8–12.

Boyer, E. L. *College: The Undergraduate Experience in America.* New York: Harper & Row, 1987.

El-Khawas, E. "Colleges Reclaim the Assessment Initiative." *Educational Record,* 1987, *68* (2), 54–58.

Ewell, P. T. (ed.). *Assessing Educational Outcomes.* New Directions for Institutional Research, no. 47. San Francisco: Jossey-Bass, 1985.

Halpern, D. F. *Student Outcomes Assessment: What Institutions Stand to Gain.* New Directions for Higher Education, no. 59. San Francisco: Jossey-Bass, 1987.

National Institute of Education, Study Group on the Conditions of Excellence in American Higher Education. *Involvement in Learning: Realizing the Potential of American Higher Education.* Washington, D.C.: U.S. Government Printing Office, 1984.

Trudy W. Banta is research professor in the Learning Research Center, and director of the FIPSE-sponsored Assessment Resource Center, at the University of Tennessee, Knoxville. She has coordinated the UTK campus instructional evaluation program since 1983.

With unprecedented national emphasis on quality and evaluation, processes and strategies for implementing and diffusing innovations and changes will receive renewed attention.

Using Change Strategies to Implement Assessment Programs

Richard I. Miller

This chapter concerns the complex and sensitive question of how to introduce new ideas and approaches into postsecondary education in ways that will facilitate their consideration and implementation. More specifically, the chapter is about how to introduce assessment policies and procedures most successfully.

Returning Interest in Change Strategies

Change in modern times has been a constant factor. For example, the processes of educational change were prominent topics for study and conversation in the mid 1960s. Programs and centers for the study of change were established, and much research and literature were generated. Higher education is currently returning to an interest in the processes of change. At every level, education in 1988 is entering an era quite different from the one we knew just five years ago, when *A Nation At Risk* (National Commission on Excellence in Education, 1983) stimulated a flurry of education activity in every state. Since this book appeared,

T. W. Banta (ed.). *Implementing Outcomes Assessment: Promise and Perils.*
New Directions for Institutional Research, no. 59. San Francisco: Jossey-Bass, Fall 1988.

educators have been focusing on ways to achieve higher quality and greater accountability. Assessment programs and ideas about assessment have become crucial elements of this activity.

State legislatures have moved aggressively to place education at the top of the agenda, and almost all have granted substantial increases in education funding at all levels. Many new programs have been developed, with assessment in the forefront. Nevertheless, the 1987 summer meeting of state governors signaled a slight but significant shift in state fiscal priorities. Interest in education will remain very high over the next few years, but voters are now also increasingly eager for new roads, urban development, technology, new enterprises, and safety and health services. Given the budget limitations in most states, pressure for increased funding to programs and services other than education will probably mean lower educational resources from state legislatures in the next few years. As a result, educators are beginning to explore ways to introduce effective programs into new settings: higher education institutions.

Strategies for successful adaptation of ideas and programs call for knowledge about the processes of change. Therefore, it is not surprising that our current intensive focus on quality and assessment has brought the topic of change processes back into prominence, as in the mid-1960s. With shifting state priorities, we may have only three to five years to exploit the heightened interest in higher education and to introduce and begin using new approaches to assessment.

Assessment and the Processes of Change

Knowledge about how to introduce assessment innovations and programs is in short supply at present. The American Association for Higher Education (AAHE) is coordinating a three-year assessment forum supported by the Fund for the Improvement of Postsecondary Education (FIPSE), and some clues about assessment and change are emerging from this promising development. Since 1986, FIPSE has also made assessment-related grants to some twenty other institutions and organizations. The AAHE's second national conference on assessment, in 1987, focused more on strategies for introducing assessment than the first conference did, in 1985, simply because in 1987 there was more to report and therefore more interest in adapting models. In her analysis of the second assessment conference, Hutchings (1987, p. 13) wrote: "The point is that assessment is now clearly in the implementation stage and campuses are looking for ways to make assessment a flexible tool suited to their own needs."

What are some unique, and complicating, factors of assessment that are relevant to the change process? The first factor is the complexity of most assessment innovations. At Northeast Missouri State University, for example, the assessment model has continued to evolve for thirteen years. Considerable differences among institutions, even in a single state, make the prospect of wholesale statewide adoption of one model more of a threat than an opportunity.

The second factor is professional sensitivity toward assessment in general. College teachers do assess their students, and they usually accept assessment of their own professional activities, but they often view larger assessment efforts with suspicion. Faculty would prefer to put people and money into their disciplines or into their own development, rather than into institutionwide assessment programs. Riesman (1958) has perceptively outlined the "intellectual veto group" function of the faculty, which has a historical basis and is a positive force to the extent that it prevents some poor ideas and proposals from succeeding.

The political sensitivity of assessment programs is different from the sensitivity of most other types of innovations. It constitutes the third factor. It may be related to professional sensitivity but can also be quite different. In terms of submerged resistance to statewide mandates, politics may operate at the professorial level or at the institutional level. Political sensitivity sometimes places the campus chief executive officer (CEO) in an uncomfortable position: between the governing board's enthusiasm for accountability and assessment, and the faculty's order of values, which may not give campuswide assessment a prominent place.

To introduce, institutionalize, and continuously modify assessment requires a commitment of time, which can be a fourth complicating factor. The average institutional tenure for CEOs, chief academic officers (CAOs), and college deans is about five years. Therefore, the multiyear span of most assessment programs probably will intersect with several changes in key administrative personnel. Changes in leadership often bring new priorities and emphases, and sometimes these significantly affect assessment programs that are already under way. Search committees may want to seek clarification of candidates' positions on assessment-related matters.

Changes in Federal, State, Institutional, and Individual Roles

Federal, state, local, and personal roles in assessment are changing rapidly. If *A Nation At Risk* was something of a "stick," the U.S. Department of Education and FIPSE have been using the "carrot" approach in administering grants and projects that focus on assessment. State officials have provided the "big stick" in many cases, mandating directions and, in some states (for example, Tennessee), also providing the "carrot" of financial incentives. Boyer, Ewell, Finney, and Mingle (1987) found that "a year ago, only a handful of states had formal initiatives labeled 'assessment.' Now two-thirds do" (p. 8).

According to El-Khawas (1987) postsecondary institutions are increasingly taking or reclaiming the assessment initiative. Most state education officials prefer that the initiative remain at that level, but they have lingering doubts about institutional persistence. Conversely, many institutions have suspicions about state-level initiatives. In addition, there is some fear that political pressure for "results" may bias state officials to expect implementation of complicated assessment programs.

The role of the individual in the assessment process should not be overlooked. Barnett (1953) views innovation as both a mental and an individual process: "All cultural changes are initiated by individuals." It is at this level that "academic gamesmanship" comes into play (pp. 15-16, 56-57). Most assessment battles are ultimately won or lost in the academic trenches, where individual faculty members live. State officials and university administrators can unwittingly lose their "feel" for the faculty perspective. Sophisticated faculty members also have ways of changing or sabotaging an assessment effort. Astin (1976, pp. 75-85) catalogues some academic games that people may play, including these:

1. *Rationalization.* This is a familiar defense mechanism, which is highly verbal and which depends heavily on abstract reasoning.
2. *Passing the buck.* A frequent method of sidetracking an issue is to form a committee or a task force to study it.
3. *Obfuscation.* One common form of this technique is to invoke platitudes or high-sounding generalizations that lead nowhere but create the impression of genuine concern and interest.
4. *Co-optation.* This method involves open acceptance of a problem, together with a suggestion that steps have already been taken to remedy it; in its extreme form, co-optation uses the assertion that the problem has already been solved.
5. *Displacement and projection.* One can try to obviate the need for serious consideration of data by citing either their inadequacies or shortcomings in the services provided by the initiator of the project or by the supplier of the data.

Astin's insightful comments about ways in which faculty members creatively avoid programs and decisions that they oppose needs to be balanced with the awareness that other faculty members who believe in a program provide the drive, insight, and imagination to see it through. Their role is crucial, and assessment directors must enlist their support to avoid the academic gamesmanship that Astin describes.

Change Models

Many models or strategies for bringing about change have been developed, and some aspects of each may be useful. Five have been chosen for brief comment here.

Commonly cited in organizational behavior books, Lewin's (1951) approach involves three steps: *unfreeze,* which refers to awareness of the need for change; *change,* which refers to movement from the old state to the new one; and *freeze,* which means operating from new premises or in new conditions.

Ryan and Gross's classical study of hybrid seed corn (1943) has inspired several change models. Ryan and Gross found three stages in the adoption process: awareness, or first hearing about the new idea; trial, or first use; and adoption, or 100 percent use. The time between awareness and complete adoption averaged about nine years for 259 farmers who had adopted hybrid corn. About five and a half years were required between awareness and trial, and three and a half years between trial and 100 percent use.

The adoption process developed by Rogers (1962) received wide attention during the mid 1960s. His model has five stages or steps: "At the *awareness* stage the individual is exposed to the innovation but lacks complete information about it. He then becomes interested in the innovation and seeks information about it at the *interest* stage. At the *evaluation* stage the individual mentally applies the innovation to his present and anticipated future situations, and then decides whether or not to try it. The individual uses the innovation on a small scale in order to determine its utility in his own situation at the *trial* stage. At the *adoption* stage the individual decides to continue the full use of the innovation" (p. 119).

Blake and Mouton (1982), writing about changing norms in an industrial setting, give these basic steps in changing norms:
1. All norms carriers actively participate.
2. Leadership is by those ultimately responsible for decisions.
3. Participants are involved who are concerned with the problem/ process.
4. Facts and data are provided about the objective situation.
5. Ventilation and catharsis are provided.
6. Reasons for current problems are identified.
7. Implicit agreements are made explicit.
8. Changes in norms are followed up.

Another model for industrial change, developed by Kirkpatrick (1985, p. 102), has seven steps: determining the need or desire for a change, preparing a tentative plan, analyzing probable reactions, making a final decision, establishing a timetable, communicating the change, and implementing the change.

These five change models have similarities as well as differences, because developers of such models start by reviewing the literature on other change models. Then they use their own perspectives, research, and experiences to develop their particular approaches.

Characteristics of a Change Model

How does one develop a change model for some phase of assessment? It is done carefully and persistently, because the prospects for
successful development and implementation of programs will be considerably diminished without a well-developed change strategy. The
approach here, rather than to outline a strategy, is to suggest developmental criteria that might be considered, on the basis of *what, why, who,
how,* and *when.*

What is the nature of your institution? At a session of the AAHE's
second national conference on assessment, a meeting attended by nearly
fifty administrators from institutions affiliated with the American Association for State Colleges and Universities, there was general head-nod-
ding to a comment that much of what has been done successfully and
admirably at Alverno College simply does not apply to other institutions.
The assessment dialogue has not always recognized the obvious and significant variable of institutional difference.

What the nature of the assessment technique or process will be
needs careful consideration; the assessment of learning outcomes, for
example, is fairly simple as compared with the development or maintenance of the value-added concept. Assessments that bring about changes
in organizational structure may have the deceptive appearance of also
changing attitudes, but changing attitudes does not necessarily change
behavior. Establishing an office for instructional development and evaluation, which may be a highly desirable change, is not in itself likely to
bring about changes in attitude or behavior concerning faculty evaluation, for example.

Why is the assessment being proposed or undertaken? Not all
changes result in improvements. In his third annual address, President
Millard Fillmore said: "It is not strange . . . that such an exuberance of
enterprise should cause individuals to mistake change for progress." The
question of *why* needs to be carefully considered, so that busy people will
commit time and energy to the enterprise.

Those who initiate or provide leadership for assessment enterprises
may benefit from regularly reminding themselves that the traditional
IBM slogan, "Think," is the main stock-in-trade of faculty members,
who represent an intelligent, curious, generally positive, slightly cynical,
and hardworking vital segment of American society. Innovators who
develop confused, unclear, or devious strategies for faculty involvement
must check their own motives as well as keep looking behind to see if
anyone is really following.

Who should be involved in an assessment program? This question
may be answered similarly at different types of institutions. The CEO's
persistence and known support are as crucial to programs in postsecon-

dary institutions as they are to programs in business organizations. Moreover, one is rarely wrong to state that persistent support by the CAO is also very important to the success of most academic innovations. This support includes spending money, overcoming constraints, making choices among alternatives on policy matters and important procedural matters, and initiating and institutionalizing academic changes. Does the institution have a history of top-down or bottom-up decision making? While institutions are rarely "either-or" in this respect, they do have tendencies in one direction or the other. Top-down tendencies rely more on vigorous support from the CEO and the CAO, without which the assessment innovation very likely would flounder and fail. A bottom-up institution relies more on faculty support; Kirkpatrick (1985, pp. 112–150) writes that the three keys to successful change are empathy, communication, and participation.

Every campus has a number of "campus influentials"—individuals who have high credibility across college and disciplinary lines. Their support of and participation in assessment are important. They may be slow to give their support and perhaps will frustrate a contingent that wants to move the program ahead. In most cases, close scrutiny by these influential people does not jeopardize externally established schedules, nor should it be judged a delaying tactic; any necessary delay is a short-term inconvenience for long-term gain. While the active, initial support of "campus influentials" can be crucial, the long-term success of the program will depend on additional factors, such as good leadership, the attractiveness of the program, timing, and the change strategies used.

Whom to involve on program committees requires careful thought beyond the involvement of influential people. For example, should the committee use representation by college or by expertise? What size is best? How should age, ethnicity, and gender be considered? What time commitment should be required of each committee member?

How should the strategy for introducing and undertaking assessment programs be developed? How one develops a strategy for assessment depends significantly on the type and nature of the institution. Community colleges, for example, may be able to move more swiftly than four-year institutions and, in exceptional cases, may serve as quiet executioners of ill-conceived, ill-timed, or poorly staffed assessment efforts. Not all assessment innovations deserve to live.

The "how" dimension includes some kind of timetable and some strategy for change. The timetable must allow sufficient time for unforeseen events. Serving as a guide, rather than as a prescription for progress, the timetable provides a useful map of new terrain. The extent of detail developed in the timetable may depend on external requirements for monitoring grants. A detailed three-year timetable may be required by the funding agency, but those who draw up such a document should seek as much flexibility as possible in its operation. Loose timetables permit leaders to cope with unexpected developments.

Strategies for change need to be designed to fit the nature of a particular institution or consortium, the governance style of the institution, the required or developed timetable, the complexity and sensitivity of the assessment, and the personalities of the innovators. These individuals tend to be more task-oriented than process-oriented. As a result, they may need to be reminded that process is at least as important as product. Assessment project directors need to develop strategies that adapt rather than adopt national models; no one has ever developed an all-purpose, universal strategy.

When is the final dimension considered here, although the sequencing of these five criteria must be adapted to particular institutions. "When" considerations may be important at the beginning; for example, individuals at a smaller institution that has just finished one regional and two national accreditation reports may be suffering from "evaluation fatigue" or motivational exhaustion and may not be ready to embark on another major assessment project. The timing of the various phases of change strategies for assessment programs requires careful thought. Again, guidelines may be softer than prescriptions, less threatening to faculty members, and structured enough to keep the project on schedule.

Success- and Failure-Prone Change Strategies for Assessment Projects

At the risk of oversimplification, these two lists of factors have been derived from the literature, as well as from practice. The lists are not intended to be inclusive, nor are the points listed in any particular logical sequence or order of importance.

Success-prone factors included the following:
- An obvious problem or need that is generally recognized as needing serious attention
- A CEO and a CAO who are fully committed to the project
- Additional available human and material resources
- Change viewed as leading to improvement
- A carefully developed plan of action widely communicated
- Appropriate faculty involvement and active participation, particularly among "campus influentials"
- Effective and efficient project leadership
- A campus climate conducive to assessment
- Credibility of the overall effort and of individuals most closely involved
- An error-expectation attitude among project leaders.

Failure-prone factors are also worthy of consideration. We very rarely admit failure in higher education, nor do we often analyze our mistakes constructively. Agriculturists analyze crop failures; doctors perform autopsies; in higher education, we write another proposal. Failure-prone strategies will include these factors:

- Weak, clandestine, or indecisive project leadership
- Insensitivity of overenthusiastic advocates
- Nominal or token support at the top
- Ambivalence not treated as normal, when there is concern about "maintenance of the way things are versus the risks and energies involved in a change effort" (Lippitt, 1985, p. 67)
- Poor timing in terms of campus morale or major academic activities
- Poorly designed plans
- Excessively complex plans
- Failure to appreciate the intricacies and complications of communication
- Failure to realize the human propensity not to change.

This condition is age-old; in 1597, Francis Bacon (1906) wrote "On Innovations," in which he observed: "It is true that what is settled by custom, though it be not good, at least it is fit. And those things which have long gone together are as it were confederate within themselves; whereas new things piece not so well; but though they help by their utility, yet they trouble by their inconformity. Besides, they are like strangers, more admired and less favored."

References

Astin, A. W. *Academic Gamesmanship: Student-Oriented Change in Higher Education.* New York: Praeger, 1976.

Bacon, F. *Essays.* London: Dent, 1906.

Barnett, H. G. *Innovation: The Basis of Cultural Change.* New York: McGraw-Hill, 1953.

Blake, R., and Mouton, J. S. *Productivity: The Human Side.* New York: Amacom, 1982.

Boyer, C. M., Ewell, P. T., Finney, J. E., and Mingle, J. R. "Assessment and Outcomes Measurement: A View from the States." *AAHE Bulletin,* 1987, *39* (7), 8–12.

El-Khawas, E. "Colleges Reclaim the Assessment Initiative." *Educational Record,* 1987, *68* (2), 54–58.

Hutchings, P. "Lessons Learned: A Report on the National Conference on Assessment in Higher Education." *AAHE Bulletin,* 1987, *40* (1), 13–14.

Kirkpatrick, D. L. *How to Manage Change Effectively: Approaches, Methods, and Case Examples.* San Francisco: Jossey-Bass, 1985.

Lewin, K. *Field Theory in Social Science.* New York: Harper & Row, 1951.

Lippitt, R. "Gaining Acceptance and Commitment to Planned Change." In D. L. Kirkpatrick, *How to Manage Change Effectively: Approaches, Methods, and Case Examples.* San Francisco: Jossey-Bass, 1985.

14

National Commission on Excellence in Education. *A Nation at Risk: The Imperative for Educational Reform*. Washington, D.C.: National Commission on Excellence in Education, 1983.

North Central Rural Sociology Committee, Subcommittee for the Study of Diffusion of Farm Practices. *How Farm People Accept New Ideas*. Ames, Iowa: Cooperative Extension in Agriculture and Home Economics, Special Report no. 15, 1962. 11 pp.

Riesman, D. *Constraint and Variety in American Education*. New York: Doubleday, 1958.

Rogers, E. M. *Diffusion of Innovations*. New York: The Free Press of Glencoe, 1962.

Ryan, B., and Gross, N. C. "Acceptance and Diffusion of Hybrid Corn Seed in Two Iowa Communities." *Rural Sociology*, 1943, *8*, 15–24.

Richard I. Miller is professor of higher education and coordinator of educational leadership at Ohio University.

*Designing assessment programs requires defining objectives
and choosing techniques. Implementing assessment, however,
is an organizational responsibility. Administration should
appropriately consider both sets of issues before embarking
on such an effort.*

Implementing Assessment:
Some Organizational Issues

Peter T. Ewell

Implementing a successful assessment program requires a fusion of three
quite different activities. First, assessment is about teaching, and neglect-
ing the instructional focus means that there is little point to the exercise.
Second, assessment is research; consequently, it demands attention to
classic researchers' questions of method, inference, and ethics. Finally,
assessment is an administrative activity. Certainly, in the early stages of
implementing assessment, organizational issues are paramount, as this
stage often involves resolving such questions as incentives and new assignments of responsibility. More important, however, assessment is about
institutional change; an ultimate objective is to help create a campus
culture that is better informed about and more conducive to improvements in teaching and learning.

    In beginning a discussion of the many organizational issues that
surround assessment, it is tempting to pose a contradiction. There is
nothing terribly new about the activity; higher education's history reveals
numerous attempts to systematically investigate the effectiveness of teaching and learning for purposes of improving instruction (Pace, 1979).
Nevertheless, there is surely something new about the way recent interest
in assessment has arisen, and the novelty exists primarily in its organizational character.

T. W. Banta (ed.). *Implementing Outcomes Assessment: Promise and Perils.*
New Directions for Institutional Research, no. 59. San Francisco: Jossey-Bass, Fall 1988.

First, recent calls for assessment have largely been external, and particularly prominent have been the escalating requirements of state governments (Boyer, Ewell, Finney, and Mingle, 1987). A major implication is that assessment is from the outset an administrative activity. Not only do administrators serve as a first point of contact and an ultimate point of responsibility for communicating assessment results, but they also are the primary initiators of what in many cases is seen as a substantial change in campus culture. Consequently, many organizational and policy issues must be resolved from the outset rather than, as was possible in the past, being allowed to evolve from experience.

Second, assessment in its current guise is programmatic. It is comprehensive, visible, and integrated. It often involves data-gathering methods of many types and requires coordination among many previously scattered offices and functions. Assessment programs generally involve an explicit and recognized administrative center. Usually they are identifiably funded through designated budgets. These features also raise explicit organizational issues: the administrative location and reporting lines for the assessment function, the structural incentives involved, and the role that assessment information should play in decision making.

Given the current nature of assessment as an administrative imperative, what specific organizational pitfalls are associated with institutional assessment, and how are institutions responding? Emerging answers are most easily discussed in terms of three broad headings that roughly correspond to the order in which, at most institutions, organizational problems are encountered and overcome. Under each heading, it is appropriate first to consider the kinds of organizational obstacles that are typically encountered and then to review briefly the kinds of remedies that seem most promising.

Initiating Assessment

Because assessment programs involve novel and often suspect bureaucratic procedures, starting them may raise many organizational difficulties. At best, assessment may be seen as unnecessary, because it duplicates existing methods of grading and program evaluation. At worst, it may be threatening, because it bypasses or disturbs carefully established faculty autonomy and accountability mechanisms. In both cases, a major cure is time. Most successful programs have started small and developed slowly. In contrast, many institutions are currently obliged to field assessment programs quickly in response to state mandates or administrative directives. As a result, the organizational problems associated with initiating assessment are particularly salient. Four seem especially noteworthy.

Unclear Motives. Too often, no one on campus is really sure what assessment is for. Usually the rhetoric of assessment is not much help, as benefits are claimed by proponents in virtually every arena. In fact, however, the structure of institutional assessment may vary markedly as a function of its basic purpose. Is the primary intent of the program to evaluate curricula? to demonstrate external accountability? to recruit, or raise funds for the institution? to change the way teaching and learning occur in individual classrooms? Answers to questions of this kind drive some fundamental elements of program design. One is the unit of analysis: Are data on individual students to be collected and maintained, or are aggregate data on a sample population sufficient? Another element is the "ownership" of information: Are assessment results to be made public, or are they to be closely held by individual faculties for their own use? Issues of this kind, although controversial, must be raised and considered from the outset. If unresolved, they will often lead to much more serious conflicts at a later point. Sometimes such issues are best resolved by explicitly stating what the program is not intended to do. A common reservation of many faculty about assessment, for example, is that the results will be used in faculty evaluation. Because of the emotion generated by this issue, considerable opposition can develop. As a result, some institutions have issued policy statements that explicitly prohibit such uses of assessment results.

Unknown Consequences. Associated with unclear motives are unknown consequences: If people do not know the actual intent of the program, they do not know quite what it is liable to do to them. In the absence of concrete information, opponents of assessment often view its consequences in "worst case" terms. A particular fear is that the institution will try to investigate every aspect of student performance. Obviously, this is seen as an endless and enormously expensive undertaking. Another fear is that instruction will be trivialized by the widespread introduction of standardized examinations: Instructors will "teach to the test" and will ignore more complex aspects of learning. Because they have heard them so many times, assessment's proponents tend to dismiss such fears out of hand, but it is important to recognize that without a clearly stated rationale for assessment, such fears are far from groundless. "Worst case" estimates, however, are usually based on very little concrete information about what has happened elsewhere. As a result, many successful programs include in the design phase considerable inquiry into what other institutions have experienced. They generally find that real programs are neither as comprehensive as proponents have claimed nor as obtrusive as opponents fear.

Lack of Visibility or Identity. Like any innovation, assessment may disturb carefully contrived (and often informal) bureaucratic relationships. It may entail reassignment of functions and responsibilities among academic affairs, student testing, the registrar, institutional research, and student affairs. More important, it may cut across traditional departmental lines and violate customary distinctions between the roles of academic and student affairs. As a result, a basic challenge for emerging assessment efforts is to establish a clear organizational identity. Sometimes the remedy is to assign responsibility to an existing office or to an individual who currently controls most of the resources needed. At other times the solution is to create a new office, with its own staff and an independent funding base. Whatever the approach, success will also require visible support from the institution's top leadership, particularly in the early stages of implementation.

Where to Start. A final problem associated with initiating assessment is also perceptual: uncertainty about how to begin such a complex undertaking. Successful programs cited in the literature are exemplary, but they often seem so complex that there is a natural tendency for those responsible for implementation to feel overwhelmed. This perception is exacerbated by the typically short timetables provided for implementation. Many observers overlook, however, the fact that most established programs began small and developed incrementally. Successful implementation may depend not only on a study of the current condition of state-of-the-art programs, but also on an examination of how these programs began and evolved.

Given these problems, what mechanisms does emerging experience suggest to overcome them? One is a new office or a specially created committee to coordinate implementation. This mechanism speaks primarily to lack of visibility, but it may also serve as a vehicle for addressing lack of clarity and uncertain objectives. Offices of this kind are generally small, employing at most one or two individuals, but they generally also report to relatively high administrative levels of authority. While their primary mission is to integrate assessment activities, their professional staff also serve as technical consultants to faculty who are attempting to develop their own assessment devices, and they also help policymakers interpret results. Perhaps most important, because they are funded and permanent, offices of this kind are symbolic of institutional commitment. In the absence of clear goals and full commitment, however, permanence can be double-edged; the creation of an office may be seen by faculty as a needless addition to an already large and unproductive administrative bureaucracy.

Special committees often serve the same kinds of functions. Virtually every recent successful implementation of assessment has begun with such a committee, generally selected carefully from among faculty opinion leaders and others whose support is needed. A major initial assignment of such committees is to compile the experiences of other institutions. At Kean College, for example, members of the committee visited other institutions and attended numerous national conferences and seminars. Only after impressions of these experiences were assembled and discussed did the committee proceed. Another common task is to prepare a policy statement or model program for the institution. Statements of this kind help to clarify what is intended and to avoid uncertainty about consequences. The statement at Kean College, for example, indicated the types of assessment devices that departments might consider, provided guidance on the kinds of instruments that were available and acceptable, and explicitly prohibited the use of assessment results in faculty evaluation (Kean College of New Jersey, 1986).

A second problem-solving mechanism is the use of pilot or demonstration projects. Unclear motives and uncertain consequences are ultimately resolved through actual experience. As a result, most successful programs have begun with a pilot phase. Generally, pilot projects are departmentally based. Selected academic units (and occasionally nonacademic units, as well) are given modest resources to undertake a range of local experiments with assessment. Pilot projects usually cover a wide range of techniques, and units are allowed considerable discretion in method. Pilots are occasionally organized as planned variations that systematically attempt a range of approaches in different settings. James Madison University, for example, used four departments in its pilot year, each of which used a different assessment approach.

Obviously, selecting appropriate pilots is an art, since one must balance technical and political considerations. From the technical standpoint, pilots should cover different kinds of departments—traditional and professional, large and small. They must also try out a range of different assessment techniques. From the political standpoint, the best pilots involve academic units that are already committed to using assessment. Because they directly benefit from the process, faculty in such units will often serve as advocates for assessment as the process becomes more widespread. Finally, if an institution is to learn from its pilot efforts, these should be carefully documented and widely publicized. The implementation process at James Madison University, for example, included a formal "showcase" conference, in which each of the four pilot departments publicly reported on its experiences.

A third problem-solving mechanism, already widely advocated in the literature on assessment, is to determine what the institution is already doing. Most colleges and universities currently engage in many activities that fall under the rubric of assessment, including entry testing of basic skills, studies of student retention and enrollment management, student surveys, alumni follow-up studies, and departmental testing. Discovering, documenting, and integrating such activities is an important initial step. When this first step has been taken, the task seems less overwhelming; some needs are already fully met, and meeting others may require the modification of an old technique more often than the design of a wholly new one.

Another way to build on current practice is to identify existing points of contact with students. Institutions already collect data from students in a number of settings. A good place to begin implementing more complex assessment procedures is to make the data-collection techniques used at these points both more sophisticated and more broadly useful. For example, most institutions require an orientation process for new students, which can be used as a convenient point to administer a pretest or a questionnaire. Most engage in course-by-course student evaluation of instruction; instruments used here can be modified to include additional items on self-reported gains in desired general education outcomes. A range of techniques is also available to use existing student "products," such as examinations, term papers, and writing exercises. Bethany College, West Virginia, for example, collects pre- and post-writing samples, both to assess student growth in writing skills and to examine attitudes about the campus environment. Other institutions are experimenting with "secondary reading" of student course examinations by committees charged with evaluating the answers collectively as evidence of growth in such qualities as critical thinking and problem solving.

From Data to Information

A second set of organizational problems may arise in the interpretation of assessment information. Indeed, institutions currently seem more beset by these difficulties than by any other. Having already made decisions about myriad data-collection processes, in response to widespread calls to get something started, they are now faced with literally mounds of data, many of which are complex, technical, and hard to interpret properly. Moreover, little thought has been given to who should do the interpreting or to how the conversion of data into useful information should be organizationally supported. This syndrome is often apparent as part of one of four typical operational problems.

The "Perfect Data" Fallacy. Because outcomes measurement is imprecise, many may feel that its implementation is not worth the effort, or at least that it should be postponed until better methods are available. Since most assessment methods are limited (as, indeed, are approaches to gathering data about anything), this rationale forms a solid basis of opposition. Moreover, it accords well with academic culture. Surely we would not want to proceed with inquiry on the basis of a flawed method. Manifestations of the "perfect data" fallacy are both plentiful and subtle and can occur at any stage of implementation. As results become available, for example, it is common for those who do not like what is found to cloak their reservations in methodological language. A few well-publicized technical limitations in the methods employed, even if their probable substantive effects are small, are often enough to call the validity of the entire enterprise into question. Another manifestation is to delay action until the "best" methods are available. For example, considerable time is wasted in attempts to locate or design one big study that will ultimately be able to answer all questions. Most rapidly discover that no such study is possible, and that it is better to start small, with a robust methodology, and to learn from the mistakes encountered. Moreover, successful practitioners generally develop methods for making crude "sensitivity estimates" of the consequences of error. In most cases, the policy judgments to be informed by assessment remain unaffected across a wide range of obtained results. Providing a rough estimate of the probable variation in obtained results on any instrument, and determining whether a given decision may change at any point across this range of variation, is a particularly useful exercise.

The "Single Indicator" Fallacy. The "perfect data" fallacy is most typical of faculty, but the "single indicator" fallacy is most typical of administrators and governing bodies. Essentially, the fallacy consists in the belief that there exists a single number, study, or approach that can answer all questions. If located, of course, a single approach is a bureaucrat's dream: It is simple, easily communicable, and probably cheap, and it allows easy choices among alternatives. Moreover, it makes assessment readily compatible with other familiar single indicators, such as cost and productivity. The problem of single indicators is most likely to arise when standardized tests are included in assessment and, consequently, when comparisons among institutions can be expected. Under such conditions, wise institutions not only will resist the tendency to make judgments on the basis of a single source but will also collect and communicate to external authorities a range of contextual information that helps to qualify or explain an obtained result (Ewell, 1987).

The "Face Validity" Problem. A third difficulty arises primarily when assessment results must be communicated to and used by nontechnical audiences. Here, assessment results not only must be valid, they must also appear valid. An excellent example is the widely used practice of sampling. Many of those to whom results are communicated simply do not believe in the validity of sample-based results. More subtly, sample-based studies often have little decisional impact, because results cannot be obtained reliably at the unit or the departmental level. Because most of the action in colleges and universities is at the departmental level, results that cannot be attributed to this level are of limited utility. As a result, a number of institutions (for example, the University of Tennessee, at Knoxville) that once extensively used samples now find it worth the investment to obtain some assessment data from all students. Of course, similar observations can be made about any other complex statistical or data-collection procedure—for example, multivariate procedures or causal models. While such tools are often invaluable for discovering a particular finding, documenting and communicating it to affected parties is generally much more effective if based on simpler approaches.

The Power of Negative Evidence. An emerging paradox also deserves mention here: Institutions fear the impact of negative findings, but emerging experience suggests that negative findings are most likely to induce positive action. Indeed, some institutions that administer such normed examinations as the ACT-COMP have admitted frustration about using the information for change, because the scores are "too good." So long as obtained scores are above the mean, it is assumed that all is well, regardless of the fact that a careful examination of subscore and subpopulation results may reveal many opportunities for improvement. Moreover, some of the most powerful documented examples of using assessment results center on the ability of negative evidence to mobilize action. Probably the classic case of this phenomenon is Northeast Missouri State University, where evidence of freshman-sophomore regression in math subscores on the ACT residual were used to guide a range of effective curricular reforms (McClain and Krueger, 1985). In itself, this phenomenon is certainly not bad; indeed, it can be claimed as the primary end of all programmatic evaluation. Nevertheless, exclusive attention to the "down side" of assessment results can produce a counterproductive attitude throughout the institution, one of avoiding scrutiny by obscuring deficiencies.

How is this particular range of organizational difficulties best overcome? Again, many techniques have proved useful. One is to develop multiple settings in which to discuss the implications of assessment results; assessment committees often play such a role. To be useful in stimulating such a dialogue, however, assessment results must be communicated in certain ways. A particular syndrome to be avoided is "data glut"—providing so much information, in so much detail, that major implications are buried. Avoiding this syndrome often involves designing data-presentation formats explicitly to provoke reactions, raise questions, and encourage further discussion (Kinnick, 1985). Data-based dialogue of this kind can also be fostered in the day-to-day tasks of assessment professionals who work with individual departments and units.

A related technique is the use of expectations exercises in conjunction with major data-collection efforts. These generally involve asking department heads, committee members, and other affected parties to systematically document what they think the pattern of results is going to look like, before the actual data are obtained. Results can be used to counter a commonly advanced objection to data collection by test or survey: that the effort will not reveal anything that is not already known. Exercises of this kind can also be undertaken as part of planning. For example, in a recent curriculum-planning retreat, faculty at Northeast Missouri State University created ideal item profiles for future years. They used a range of currently employed assessment instruments and relied on actual historical data as a base (Northeast Missouri State University, 1987). Results of the expectations exercise can be used both as a guide to action and as a template against which to evaluate actual future data.

A third technique is to center discussion of assessment results on a particular identified problem or constituency. Again, this is old advice, verified across a range of projects on data utilization (Ewell, 1984). For assessment, however, it may prove particularly valuable in overcoming discrepant methodologies and fragmented administrative responsibilities. Integrating the results of such diverse data-collection processes as student surveys, interviews, and behavioral tests may seem overwhelming if all phenomena are deemed of equal importance. A particular problem or constituency orientation can help focus such efforts by giving them a clear agenda. One working group of the recently established Harvard Assessment Seminar, for example, is concentrating on the bottom quarter of the undergraduate population; a series of integrated investigations is planned, with this constituency as the primary target. A specific focus also helps in implementing recommendations once the implications of available data have been made clear. Often the need for action will involve the coordinated initiatives of a number of quite different offices and individuals, most of whom have little regular contact. Creating a problem-based task force consisting of such individuals can be of considerable value from the outset in inducing action. Indeed, productive and coordinated action to address the problem may not wait until formal recommendations are developed. Because affected parties with decision-making responsibility are included in task forces, improvements can often be made unilaterally.

From Information to Improvement

A third class of problems is perhaps the most difficult to overcome. These problems involve the actual use of assessment results to make appropriate changes in instruction and support services. Such problems are almost completely organizational and are generally of two kinds.

First, assessment results in themselves rarely suggest what actions are needed, partly because the methods employed are imprecise and complex. At most, they may indicate the phenomena they attempt to detect; rarely are they actively diagnostic. Most assessment methods, moreover, are sufficiently error-laden that their interpretation is ambiguous; results must generally be confirmed from a number of different sources before firm conclusions are warranted. Perhaps more important, the actual phe-

nomena toward which assessment is directed—teaching and learning—
are themselves complex and multicausal.

These factors practically ensure that any given piece of information will rarely be directly related to a particular policy decision. Indeed, institutional experience suggests that such information is often utilized in ways quite distinct from the methods of "pure" decision making (Kinnick, 1985). One alternative use of information is simply to signal the existence of a problem. Most institutional testing schemes—particularly those that rely on standardized examinations or large cross-sectional surveys—are of this variety. Such approaches are usually too imprecise to determine the cause of a deficiency, but at least they can document its presence, site, and approximate magnitude. Another nontraditional use of assessment information is to set the context for an entire range of decisions. Student survey information can be particularly helpful in this regard. Such information is often useful for gaining broad insights into student perceptions. Such insights might broadly inform decisions ranging from academic advising to the structure of student housing units. Finally, assessment information is often particularly useful in selling a decision once it has been taken. Because it is concrete, such information can be extremely effective in communicating needs and priorities to those (often outside the institution) responsible for making resource-allocation decisions. Northeast Missouri State University, for example, recently used declines in student ratings of the library as part of a successful capital budget request to support needed improvements in library facilities.

Second, assessment information is not easy to incorporate into such processes as budgeting, curriculum approval and review, and academic policymaking when these are already firmly established, partly because assessment results are often difficult for lay administrators to interpret and apply. Such information lacks the apparent simplicity of the cost or workload information to which decision makers are accustomed. More important, the collection and dissemination of assessment information is often organizationally isolated. In the absence of such integrative mechanisms as program review, units responsible for assessment have no assigned roles in the regular process of decision making.

In practice, these two kinds of difficulties are almost completely intertwined. How can they be overcome? One method is to explicitly use assessment information in planning and budgeting decisions. Tennessee's performance-funding concept, although it is a state approach, illustrates one alternative: Information is used to determine "effective" performance, which is then rewarded through supplementary funding (Banta, 1986). Institutional budgeting schemes to reward unit performance on similar grounds are currently being tried at several institutions. A contrasting example, more consistent with the use of assessment information for improvement, is to use of the information as a general guide to resource allocation. Here, information is used to identify specific programmatic needs that can be met by additional funding or to identify strategic opportunities that the institution can exploit. In both situations, assessment information does not supplant other kinds of information in determining priorities, nor do the results in themselves determine the outcome of a given decision.

A second method is to incorporate assessment information into local program reviews or evaluation processes. Information on student performance is increasingly sought through such processes. Information on student placement is most commonly used as an indicator of academic program effectiveness. Whenever it is applicable, information about student performance on professional licensing or certification examinations is also collected. Growing numbers of institutional reviews also require some kind of student opinion data. Similarly, user-satisfaction data are often sought in reviews of nonacademic support units, particularly if they have direct contact with students. Only rarely, to date, is information on the performance of current or graduating students collected, although a main feature of recent proposals to create campuswide assessment programs has been achievement testing in the major field. Such data have been collected in Tennessee for a long time, of course, and the results have proved particularly applicable to program review (Banta, 1986).

A major advantage of embedding assessment results in program review is that the information is put into the hands of those most responsible for making improvements. Research on the impact of program review strongly indicates that much of its benefit occurs immediately through self-study, long before results are officially disseminated or acted upon (Harpel, 1986; Harcleroad, 1985). At the same time, program review provides an important link to resources. Because results are often used to guide an institution's strategic investment decisions, if assessment information is explicitly included, the likelihood of its being used to inform major decisions is enhanced. Finally, program review provides a communication link both up and down the institution's administrative hierarchy. By including assessment information in their review, academic programs are guaranteed a channel through which to communicate their strengths and needs. By requiring assessment information, administrators send a consistent signal: Instructional effectiveness is a priority that will be actively investigated and rewarded.

A final organizational point of attack is to build assessment into ongoing processes for curriculum approval or review. This is particularly important in considering general education, an area not adequately addressed by unit-specific processes like program review. Many institutions are currently revising their approaches to general education. Sometimes this task involves implementing entirely new curricula. Here, explicit consideration of assessment issues has proved valuable: Assessment can be used simultaneously as a tool to determine the effects of new instructional approaches and as an important building block of the curriculum itself. Integrative comprehensive examinations, pre- and post-testing of intellectual skills, portfolio analyses, and student journals are prominent in the general education efforts of institutions as diverse as King's College, Kean College of New Jersey, and California Polytechnic State University. At most colleges and universities, however, general education reform concentrates on tightened structural requirements for course distribution across disciplines. Here, the primary challenge to curricular architects is to decide on a common set of outcomes that distributed coursework is intended to produce. In such cases, explicit consideration of assessment issues from the outset also helps avoid many fruitless and circular discussions.

Information and Institutional Change

The argument of this chapter is that administrative focus on institutional change is perhaps the most important and neglected area of the emerging assessment movement. While considerable attention is paid to the technical merits of particular assessment methods, relatively few discussions address the many organizational problems involved in actually fielding an institutional assessment program. Indeed, it may be helpful to end with the thought—somewhat heretical in the rhetoric of assessment—that the actual information that results may not be assessment's most crucial benefit. Substantive improvements in instruction can certainly be linked with particular insights gained through assessment; just as many beneficial innovations, however, appear to occur simply as results of processes that force clear thinking about curricular objectives. There are numerous examples of faculty who are willing to make important changes in curriculum, not as a result of the information collected but as a result of assessment design. Moreover, institutions like Northeast Missouri State University would be among the first to admit that an intended benefit of assessment is to mobilize opinion, both inside and outside the institution. Such examples (somewhat akin to the classic Hawthorne effect of experimental design) suggest that assessment may pay its greatest long-term dividends as an organizational device for directing scarce reserves of institutional attention away from other concerns and toward the neglected area of teaching and learning.

This observation leads to a final point about implementation, one that at the organizational level roughly parallels Astin's (1985) notion of involvement as a key to individual learning. In essence, Astin argues that no particular instructional or campus experience is ultimately responsible for producing gains in student learning; what is more important is the degree to which these experiences act in concert to produce a climate of active involvement. Involvement is also important at the organizational level. Many observers of assessment have noted that high levels of participation among faculty and line administrators in designing, piloting, and implementing programs is a primary key to success but efforts to achieve organizational involvement cannot be attempted in piecemeal fashion. Instead, these efforts demand application of what might be termed (in parallel with the Astin's notion of involvement) the "theory of administrative consistency."

Consistency demands that actions be consciously organized. Although they are carried out by many units across the campus, assessment activities should have a clear and articulated common purpose. More important, consistency demands that the organizational incentives surrounding assessment be properly aligned. If units are expected to participate wholeheartedly, they must be given the necessary resources. Moreover, the institution must ensure that older, traditional incentive structures do not continue to reward noncooperation. Most important of all, consistency demands that the institution's leaders support their rhetoric with visible action. To faculty who participate in good faith and at some cost, in the expectation that identified needs will be met, there are few experiences more frustrating than to see the results of their assessment efforts ignored and to watch resources being allocated on a timeworn incremental or political basis. To avoid such an outcome, administrators must demonstrate respect for the assessment process in all spheres of activity, even though it may considerably constrain their own latitude for decision making. If respect of this kind is absent, the implementation of assessment will quickly become what its critics rightly fear—an empty and burdensome bureaucratic exercise.

References

Astin, A. W. *Achieving Educational Excellence: A Critical Assessment of Priorities and Practices in Higher Education*. San Francisco: Jossey-Bass, 1985.

Banta, T. W. (ed.). *Performance Funding in Higher Education: A Critical Analysis of Tennessee's Experience*. Boulder, Colo.: National Center for Higher Education Management Systems, 1986.

Boyer, C. M., Ewell, P. T., Finney, J. E., and Mingle, J. R. "Assessment and Outcomes Measurement: A View from the States." *AAHE Bulletin*, 1987, *39* (7), 8–12.

Ewell, P. T. *The Self-Regarding Institution: Information for Excellence*. Boulder, Colo.: National Center for Higher Education Management Systems, 1984.

Ewell, P. T. *Assessment, Accountability, and Improvement: Managing the Contradiction*. Washington, D.C.: American Association for Higher Education, 1987.

Harcleroad, F. F. "The Context of Academic Program Evaluation." In E. C. Craven (ed.), *Academic Program Evaluation*. New Directions for Institutional Research, no. 27. San Francisco: Jossey-Bass, 1985.

Harpel, R. L. *The Anatomy of an Academic Program Review*. Tallahassee, Fla.: Association for Institutional Research, 1986.

28

Kean College of New Jersey. *A Proposal for Program Assessment at Kean College of New Jersey: Final Report of Presidential Task Force on Student Learning and Development.* Union: Kean College of New Jersey, 1986.

Kinnick, M. K. "Increasing the Use of Student Outcomes Information." In P. T. Ewell (ed.), *Assessing Educational Outcomes.* New Directions for Institutional Research, no. 47. San Francisco: Jossey-Bass, 1985.

McClain, C. J., and Krueger, D. W. "Using Outcomes Assessment: A Case Study in Institutional Change." In P. T. Ewell (ed.), *Assessing Educational Outcomes.* New Directions for Institutional Research, no. 47. San Francisco: Jossey-Bass, 1985.

Northeast Missouri State University. *Five-Year Planning Document.* Kirksville: Northeast Missouri State University, 1987.

Pace, C. R. *Measuring Outcomes of College: Fifty Years of Findings and Recommendations for the Future.* San Francisco: Jossey-Bass, 1979.

Peter T. Ewell is senior associate with the National Center for Higher Education Management Systems.

*Documentation of what students learn, instead of only their
relative levels of performance, is at the heart of any effective
assessment of educational quality.*

Cognitive Measures
in Assessing Learning

Jonathan Warren

Cognitive measures play a limited but crucial role in educational assessment. They are defined here as procedures for observing and recording
students' intellectual accomplishments. The information they provide
should inform students about what they have and have not learned, faculty members about the successes and failures of their instruction, and
department heads and deans about the suitability of the curriculum in
bringing students to the desired academic capabilities. The first of these
functions requires information about individual students; the other two,
information about collective learning.

The Cognitive Complexity of Learning

In the past several decades, cognitive science has grown dramatically as a discipline and as a context in which to examine and perhaps
restructure education. One point on which cognitive scientists agree is
that knowledge and cognitive skills, or methods of using and manipulat-
ing knowledge, are both necessary components of successful intellectual
activity (Gardner, 1985; Simon, 1980). A second point of agreement is
that cognitive or intellectual activities are numerous and diverse: "Even
if the processes by which individuals reason or classify may be similar

T. W. Banta (ed.). *Implementing Outcomes Assessment: Promise and Perils.*
New Directions for Institutional Research, no. 59. San Francisco: Jossey-Bass, Fall 1988.

the world over, the actual products and *the ways they are thought about* may be so different as to make illuminating generalizations elusive" (Gardner, 1985, p. 357; emphasis added). The failure of educators to settle on common goals for the teaching of thinking is understandable (Nickerson, Perkins, and Smith, 1985).

Although there can be only slippery generalizations about the most useful cognitive processes or domains of learning in the undergraduate years, attempts to grasp such generalizations are frequent. A common response to recent criticism of higher education's fragmented curricula has been to construct new "core" curricula that incorporate general intellectual goals—problem solving, historical consciousness, global awareness, analytical reasoning, and other broad rubrics that have not often served as explicit goals of instruction. As those goals are introduced into existing courses and curricula, methods for evaluating their impacts on student learning are needed; yet their variety, in both content and processes, creates problems in assessing how well students reach them.

The Gap in Information About Learning

The assessment of students' learning has remained strangely out of step with the growing complexity of that learning. Only the rare institution, such as Alverno College, has any record of the substance of what its students have learned (Alverno College Faculty, 1985). Typically, the only record related to learning is the list of courses students took and the grades they received. Grades indicate students' comparative levels of accomplishment of unspecified kinds of learning, relative to the unknown achievement of anonymous groups of other students. No adequate evaluation can be made, nor record kept, of the success of an educational enterprise without information about the substantive learning of its students—their knowledge of content and their facility with advanced cognitive processes.

The simple convenience of grades and test scores gives them great appeal; their cost, in terms of loss of meaning when widely diverse kinds of performance are forced onto a single scale, tends to be ignored. Grades represent a mix of different kinds of knowledge, cognitive skills, personal qualities or work habits, and faculty emphases. Nevertheless, these components are all presumed equivalent when a student's performance is placed on a one-dimensional scale of achievement. Standardized tests have the same one-dimensional quality, purposely built into them for high reliability. However widely an achievement test's items sample the domain of a field, the resulting score is based on the assumption that the items contribute to a single, uniform dimension of knowledge or ability. For some purposes, such as for indicating which applicants are best prepared for admission to an educational program, that assumption is acceptable; a general picture of academic preparation can be conveyed without providing details. In contrast, when the information's purpose is to provide a record of what students have accomplished in a program, and when that record is used by faculty, administrators, and external constituencies, the details of the learning and their variations become important. Grades may be acceptable as general indicators of relative academic success, but for evaluating the specific success of a particular educational program, more informative indicators are needed. We take pride in students who achieve academic honors, but we can seldom say in any detail what these students accomplished that other students did not. If a group of foreign professors visiting an American university were to ask about the accomplishments of, say, its history graduates, the only information they could be given would be impressionistic. The local faculty members could describe what they hoped their students would accomplish and the usual degree of student success, but they would have nothing to document or demonstrate those accomplishments. If pressed, or if embarrassed by their inability to show any evidence of what their students had learned, the faculty might bring out syllabi, textbooks, or sample examinations, but these would only indicate expectations for learning; nothing would describe what typical students in those courses had actually learned or what the more capable students had learned beyond what was typical. Some of the host faculty members might then describe their grade distributions, pointing out that almost 50 percent of the history majors got B's or better in their history courses, 50 percent C's, and only 1 or 2 percent D's and F's. Yet some of the host history faculty might find those figures embarrassing, thinking that more than half the history majors should have history grade point averages above C. Others might take pride in the same information, seeing as evidence of the department's rigor that not even half the students averaged better than C. In fact, however, grade distributions have no known reference points and no one substantive interpretation; they say nothing about the quality of learning, in terms of either content or cognitive skills.

The seriousness of the gap in information about what students learn is illustrated in a recent article on engineering education (Kerr and Pipes, 1987). The authors argue that undergraduate engineering education has declined over the past thirty years because engineering curricula have shifted their emphases from the poorly defined problems typical of engineering practice (which often require intuitive rather than analytical approaches) to the analytical methods of theoretical science. Graduating engineers today, they claim, are less able to handle typical engineering problems than former graduates were. Their evidence comes from comparisons of college catalogues and textbooks, from which only limited inferences can be drawn about what engineering students learn. Whether current engineering graduates are actually less able to solve poorly defined problems than former graduates were can be known only from the percentages of engineering students today and in previous years who have worked successfully with various kinds of problems. To be complete, that information should describe variations in student achievement in terms of cognitive processes required to solve the problems, as well as in terms of content; neither kind of information appears in catalogues or textbooks.

Monitoring trends in the content, strengths, and weaknesses of the educational product is part of using assessment to demonstrate accountability to external constituencies, but information on the substance of what students have learned also has other uses. The special strengths of similar programs, or of courses that differ in their emphases, can be identified. Several courses' combined effects on student learning can be disentangled from their individual effects. The effects of different kinds of educational preparation for a program can be separated from the effects of the program itself. Differences between what ordinary students learn and what the best students learn can suggest modifications of instruction to accommodate students who have distinct purposes or abilities. Indicators that lack information on what was learned cannot adequately serve purposes such as these.

Sources of Information on Learning

In the following discussion, the phrase *indicators of learning* refers to the collective learning of groups of students, which is assumed to be reportable beyond the boundaries of those groups. A professor who observes that a student's oral or written report shows particularly keen understanding of a complex issue, and who reports that to the student, is engaging in the gathering and reporting of information about student learning. Similar observations of other students, if cumulated into a summary statement of the students' collective performance, would contribute to an indicator of learning, as the term is used here.

Course Examinations. The periodic examinations faculty members give their classes—quizzes, midterms, and finals—overwhelm all other sources of information on learning, in terms of time and effort given them. Those examinations have strengths most other indicators lack. First, they are directly related to the material studied. Even when wide agreement exists about the content of an undergraduate field, as in chemistry, every department has its own strengths and areas of emphasis, which are often not adequately represented in exams prepared outside the courses in which the material is taught. Second, the frequency of exams in each course makes them more comprehensive of the material covered than any so-called comprehensive exam given only at the end of an academic year. Third, they permit timely feedback about where students have succeeded and where further effort is needed. Fourth, they perform the same function for the faculty, providing information on students' difficulties soon enough for instructors to help. Fifth, they avoid the pressures of comprehensive exams, which some students find intimidating. Sixth, exams in a course usually elicit students' best efforts, but that is not always true with end-of-year exams given for the benefit of the institution. Finally, course exams require no additional time outside regular course activities from either faculty or students.

Course exams do have weaknesses, particularly if the information is to be used outside a particular course. First, as noted above, course exams rarely leave any record of what students have learned. Second, they provide no reference group against which collective learning (whether substantive or not) in a particular course or program can be compared. Much of the meaning of test results is lost in the absence of suitable reference groups. If a large proportion of students in a course get every question on an exam right, no one can be sure whether the test was too easy and the course undemanding, or whether the students were particularly capable and had learned the material unusually well. Faculty members can and do compare performances of current and past classes, but they rarely know what similar students in similar courses at other institutions have accomplished. Their expectations may be unnecessarily low or unrealistically high. Moreover, even the information that does let faculty make sense of their students' test results is often left unrecorded. Finally, course exams are often justifiably criticized for testing only what is tested easily, but often not well. The higher cognitive skills essential to academic success are sometimes difficult to observe. This is a universal problem in the assessment of learning, however, and whether it applies more severely to course exams than to other forms of assessment is questionable. If the exercise of higher cognitive skills depends on their substantive content, then faculty members are in a better position than external testing agencies to assess them. Many faculty members make good tests. Improving their test-making skills, when necessary, is not difficult.

Informal, Course-Based Observations. Apart from the formal assignments and examinations that faculty members give students, and the papers, reports, and test results that students give to their professors, there is a variety of less formal kinds of communication between faculty and students. The approach that faculty members take to a topic, the questions they raise and pursue, the kinds of assignments they give, and the attitudes they convey—through these and more subtle cues—tell perceptive students not only which issues are important but also the reasons for their importance. The questions students ask, the comments they make, and even their body language are all cues to learning that faculty members pick up (Rice, 1987). These observations are usually unsystematic, intuitive, and unrecorded, yet their results often influence grades; and grades, with all their limitations, are the most important record of learning now used.

Except in large classes, faculty members rarely have difficulty knowing which students are understanding the material, picking up the fine points, and incorporating them into an integrated understanding of a course. Faculty also know which students do the assignments, study the material regularly but mechanically, miss subtle connections among a course's concepts and issues, and leave with an acceptable grade but with only a superficial grasp of what a course was about.

The informal, intuitive sources of information that faculty members in small classes use for evaluating their students can be made more systematic and used in large as well as small classes. Faculty members can often translate the informal indicators of learning that they use intuitively into one- to five-minute written exercises, given to students at the beginning or the end of class. The results can be examined quickly for indications of where the class collectively lags in understanding or completely misses the point. At the end of the term, those collective results, briefly recorded, can constitute a detailed and virtually continual documentation of the development of understanding among the students in the course and of the variations in their collective accomplishment.

Locally Developed Comprehensive Examinations. Comprehensive exams developed by an institution for its own use are one alternative to course exams for documenting what students have learned. They may be given at the end of each academic year, at the end of the sophomore and senior years, or on completion of a program. They may be written or oral; composed of multiple-choice questions, essay questions, quantitative problems, or mixes of these; or focused on learning in the students' major fields or on general education. They may be observed and graded by local faculty, or by experts from other institutions or from outside higher education (Fong, 1987; O'Neill, 1983).

Whether comprehensive exams are developed within or outside an institution, persons other than those who taught the students usually assess them. This procedure can remove the "conflict of interest" held to exist when the instructor sets the standards, instructs the students, and evaluates their performance. It may also improve learning by allowing students and faculty to be collaborators rather than adversaries in learning. Yet the adversarial relationship is fostered more by the assignment of grades than by the examination process itself. When exams are used only as sources of information, for students and for faculty, about the substance and level of learning that has occurred, then the adversarial nature of the relationship is diminished.

Comprehensives may introduce students to perspectives on course material that differ from those of their instructors. That result, although it is unfair to students if it is used to evaluate them individually, can be valuable to the institution if it indicates portions of the curricula that have been unintentionally slighted. Developed at the students' own institution, comprehensives can be kept relevant to local curriculum and simultaneously separate assessment from teaching.

Removing assessment from individual courses has another potential advantage: Comprehensive exams may be designed to indicate how well students have integrated the learning from several courses or incorporated experiences from outside courses. Comprehensive exams provide an opportunity for documenting the synergistic effects courses are hoped to have.

Whether local or external, comprehensives have inherent weaknesses. They cannot realistically cover the entire scope of student learning, even when given each academic year. Coming at the end of a year, their results cannot be used as guides to study or instruction. They are costly in terms of student and faculty time. Finally, if they have any effect on students' academic standing, the resulting pressure on students is liable to bias the results, but if they do not affect grades, some students will not take them seriously.

One of the strengths claimed for comprehensives is that they indicate what students have really learned, rather than what they have learned just long enough to pass an exam, but that may be another weakness: Some of what students have learned a few months before the comprehensive will have been forgotten by the time the exam is given but could quickly be relearned should the need arise. Thus, comprehensives may not show some prior learning, but that does not mean the learning has been lost.

Other weaknesses, although not inherent, require careful circumvention. The material covered in comprehensives, in addition to being "uncomprehensive," may be uneven and haphazard, largely because so much material must be covered in so little time. Further, the learning that students demonstrate is rarely recorded, whether the exams are oral or written. Particularly if exams are oral, their scope, relevance, and validity may all be questionable.

An irony in the use of comprehensive exams is that their results typically take the form of a single grade. Assessment results that leave no record of the substance of learning, putting the record they do leave in a form suitable only for one-dimensional learning, are hardly comprehensive.

Externally Developed Comprehensive Examinations. Comprehensive exams developed outside an institution differ from locally developed comprehensives. The most important differences are the external exams' systematic coverage of the most common areas of a field and their provision of an independent reference group for interpreting results. Externally developed exams are usually multiple-choice tests devised by commercial testing agencies or state agencies. Comprehensive oral exams are occasionally conducted by persons from outside an institution, but they are more similar to locally developed than to external comprehensives, since they follow locally developed guidelines.

Multiple-choice exams tend to be technically well constructed, with high reliability in the form of internal consistency—that is, high interitem agreement—but that reliability makes these tests less valid as indicators of accomplishment across complex areas of learning. Even in well-specified fields like organic chemistry or mechanical engineering, competence does not consist of any uniform body of knowledge, understanding, and intellectual capabilities, which every competent person in the field can be assumed to possess. Nevertheless, such assumptions underlie tests that have high internal consistency. The variety and the complexity of learning in any field, even among graduates in highly structured fields, are too great to be accommodated by a test that assumes a single dimension of competence.

The provision of a reference group, which gives institutions a yardstick against which the performance of their own students can be measured, is also an illusory benefit. The characteristics of the students and institutions that constitute the reference group are seldom even known, and this lack of information makes comparisons questionable.

Commercially developed tests of such general academic skills as critical thinking and problem solving have become more popular with growing attention to general education. They are similar to commercial tests of achievement in subject-matter fields. Faculty members, however, are less sure of what constitutes something like critical thinking or problem solving than of what makes up the content of their own fields, and they look for expert help; but lack of agreement among the experts, as well as the interdependence between knowledge and cognitive processes, raise doubts about the superiority of external tests of general skills over locally developed tests.

Promising Prospects

Several related trends are apparent. The most obvious is the growing expectation of legislatures, governing boards, and academic administrators for information on students' academic accomplishments to be made available. At present, few constraints are placed on the forms that such information should take. The virtual absence, however, of any information on the substance of student learning (except at the occasional institution like Alverno College) is unlikely to be ignored for long.

Several years ago, colleges and universities responded to the pressure for assessment of students' learning by looking to external test developers. The trend among institutions now seems to favor relying more on their own ability to assess the learning they want their own students to demonstrate. Greater interest in short-essay tests and free-response problems, rather than in multiple-choice tests, is accompanying that shift to local resources. As faculty members shift their purposes in examining students' performance from assigning grades to investigating the substantive and cognitive effects of instruction, they will begin to engage in the kind of instructional research Cross (1986) has urged them to adopt.

Retreat from external test development accompanies a tendency among neighboring institutions to pool assessment efforts. Collaboration can lead to better specification of instructional objectives and more accurate assessment. Faculty members teaching courses with overlapping goals can include a few common questions on their retrospective exams and have accessible, identifiable reference groups to compare performances among students.

Institutions concerned with students' collective learning need not test every student on the same material. A department can organize the core of its program—the key kinds of understanding, capabilities, and appreciations required into 120 ten-minute exercises (a daunting 20-hour test). To make such time requirements more manageable, three of the exercises can be incorporated into the final exams of each of 40 upper-division courses in several fields. If some redundancy is built into the exercises and if the upper-division courses are chosen carefully, the results can indicate students' accomplishments accurately and comprehensively (including variations within the same field of study and across different fields). Collaboration of several neighboring institutions can extend the usefulness of results while distributing the costs of test development.

There should be continual interplay among the processes of clarifying instructional purposes, devising assessment exercises to reflect them, observing results, improving instruction to meet revised purposes, sharpening purposes and assessment exercises, and so on. Alverno College's elaborate but decentralized assessment program clearly demonstrates that interplay (Alverno College Faculty, 1985). With such a process, neither teaching nor learning remains stagnant, and changes and accomplishments are documented.

Potential Perils

Separating assessment from instruction has advantages as well as risks. Students may see an assessment program that is not directly related to their courses as an unnecessary burden, and faculty members may find little value in the program's results. If so, the program will be abandoned as a sterile process, and more promising attempts to assess what students have learned will have trouble getting accepted.

Few major changes in curricula or academic procedures occur without the involvement of faculty committees, yet that form of faculty involvement is often not enough; the committee perspective is too general. Committees tend to draft new statements of educational goals and then work from them toward the selection or construction of assessment devices. These goal statements, with their related assessment procedures, tend to be so broad that they have little direct bearing on courses that are currently taught. Such a procedure implies that what has already been taught and assessed is not in itself an appropriate guide to what should be done, and faculty members are reluctant to embrace the results of assessments conducted in this way.

A more productive approach is to examine what faculty members already assess, how they do it, and how closely the results reflect their expectations for student learning. That process will probably suggest clarification and restatement of purposes. It may also indicate purposes that are inadequately assessed or suggest improved or expanded assessment procedures, but the recommendations will have grown from and respected faculty members' previous efforts.

The introduction of a wholly new, externally devised assessment process is rarely necessary and is often self-defeating. An assessment program that builds on what already exists not only can provide better information than a new one on the quality of education but also can be linked more readily to the improvement of teaching and learning.

References

Alverno College Faculty. *Assessment at Alverno College.* (Rev. ed.) Milwaukee, Wisc.: Alverno Productions, 1985.

Cross, K. P. "A Proposal to Improve Teaching." *AAHE Bulletin,* 1986, *39* (1), 9-14.

Fong, B. "The External Examiner Approach to Assessment." Paper commissioned by the American Association for Higher Education at the second National Conference on Assessment in Higher Education, Denver, June 14-17, 1987.

Gardner, H. *The Mind's New Science: A History of the Cognitive Revolution.* New York: Basic Books, 1985.

Kerr, A. D., and Pipes, R. B. "Why We Need Hands-On Engineering Education." *Technology Review,* 1987, *90* (7), 34-42.

Nickerson, R. S., Perkins, D. N., and Smith, E. E. *The Teaching of Thinking.* Hillsdale, N.J.: Erlbaum, 1985.

O'Neill, J. P. "Examinations and Quality Control." In J. R. Warren (ed.), *Meeting the New Demand for Standards.* New Directions for Higher Education, no. 43. San Francisco: Jossey-Bass, 1983.

Rice, E. "Education as a Human and Humane Affair." *Liberal Education,* 1987, *73* (3), 14-21.

Simon, H. A. "Problem Solving and Education." In D. T. Tuma and F. Reif (eds.), *Problem Solving and Education: Issues in Teaching and Research.* Hillsdale, N.J.: Erlbaum, 1980.

Jonathan Warren consults with colleges and universities on ways to document their students' learning. Before becoming an independent consultant, he conducted research on undergraduate education at Educational Testing Service.

Stating specific educational objectives reduces the complexity of deciding which of a bewildering array of potential noncognitive outcomes are worth the risks and costs associated with their administration.

Use of Noncognitive Measures in Assessment

Oscar T. Lenning

Cognitive learning is the dominant outcome being assessed today, with cognitive measures emphasized, but noncognitive measures are also important for assessing cognitive criteria. They should not be overlooked, especially if we consider the diverse teaching goals that guide this country's system of higher education.

As a concept, the idea of formal assessment involving perceptive observation of both cognitive and noncognitive outcomes can probably be traced back 2,000 years, to Socrates and the Socratic method. Almost 2,000 years later, in the early years of higher education in this country—with emphasis on developing cultured gentlemen, societal leaders, and clergy—the emphasis was as much on the noncognitive as on the cognitive. Furthermore, in this century up to the present, there remains a strong goals emphasis in higher education, on both the noncognitive and the cognitive. Ewell's (1984, p. 33) classification of outcomes dimensions illustrates this emphasis.

A survey of the literature on educational outcomes and goals since the early 1900s (Lenning, 1977) identified eighty-nine distinct classifications, only eight of which focused primarily on cognitive outcomes. One primary purpose of college education is to prepare students for careers and occupations. Fine (1986, p. 68) lists forty-two critical performance

T. W. Banta (ed.). *Implementing Outcomes Assessment: Promise and Perils.*
New Directions for Institutional Research, no. 59. San Francisco: Jossey-Bass, Fall 1988.

categories, derived by analysis of ten professional jobs in the U.S. Department of Housing and Urban Development. The primary components of all forty-two of these skills are by nature noncognitive.

We can say that college professors usually do not attempt to measure intended noncognitive outcomes (if we assume that noncognitive goal statements and professors' intentions are sufficient evidence that such outcomes are receiving attention). Nevertheless, submitting "claims" as evidence of noncognitive outcome accomplishment, whether in the classroom or at a more aggregate level, will no longer be sufficient, given the growing expectations of accountability. Potential for formally collecting helpful information on such outcomes does exist, and that possibility will be a focus of this chapter.

Traditional Noncognitive Measures of Educational Outcomes

Researchers in many disciplines have long used noncognitive measures as primary data-gathering methods to help them assess educational outcomes. The six methods discussed in this chapter are broadly used across the entire curriculum.

Observable Performance Measures. Many disciplines employ internships, work samples, and group problem-solving exercises as assessment techniques. Projects, oral presentations, and debates are also widely used. Photos, slides, movies, videotapes, demonstrations, and observer checksheets can also be used to collect data. The person making the assessment may be a participant-observer (and therefore rely on an intrusive measure) or solely an external observer (whose objectivity is therefore increased, to strengthen focus on the assessment). One advantage of direct observation is that it can be a curriculum-based learning method fully as much as an assessment method; the learning and assessment occur at the same time, supplementing and supporting each other. The Student Learning Outcomes Task Force (1980) referred to such measures as "curriculum-embedded performances."

Berk (1986) draws on research in business, education, industry, the military, and psychology to discuss the advantages and disadvantages of alternative performance-assessment methods. Examples of the three dozen techniques discussed by Berk are graphic rating scales, behaviorally anchored rating scales, work-sample tests, miniature job-training and job-assessment tests, leaderless group discussion, in-basket techniques, chart audits, spontaneous performance assessments, utility analysis, and performance-distribution assessment.

Self-Report Measures. Students and alumni can provide self-reports. Alumni reports may emphasize two relevant types of information: perceptions of student experiences and the impact of those experiences, and reports of current status, activities, and accomplishments. Bard (1976) has noted that students report their perceptions honestly, even when dealing with sensitive matters. Methods for obtaining student self-reports include such self-monitoring activities as keeping diaries or journals. Oral and written presentations also summarize such results. Although the use of student portfolios can be considered a performance measure, portfolios, as "track records" of activity and accomplishment, also fit logically into the self-report category. They must be carefully designed and organized, however, if they are to show outcomes adequately.

Report charts, checklists, polls, and rating forms constitute a second category of self-report instruments. Even student ratings of courses or instructors can be used to assess educational outcomes. Published questionnaires can be helpful if the outcomes information they collect is needed locally. If an instrument is not available to measure desired outcomes specifically, consideration may be given to developing a modified version of an available instrument or developing one's own. Because of economy and the potential for better quality with less effort, modifying an existing instrument is preferable to creating a new one.

Questionnaire development is a sophisticated task, with potential pitfalls for the inexperienced or unwary. Careful attention to Edwards (1957), Oppenheim (1966), Payne (1951), Sudman and Bradburn (1982), Whitney (1972), and Berdie, Anderson, and Niebuhr (1986) can prevent unclear, complex, vague, and unfocused wording. Furthermore, how a questionnaire is administered is just as important as its design. Careless administration can destroy an outstanding design.

Interviews, which are variants of questionnaires, can be formal or informal and conducted individually, in groups, in person, or by telephone. Interviews can also now be conducted through interactively linked computers. It is important that interview questions be formulated carefully, as cues. Materials available for help in designing and conducting interviews include Guba and Lincoln's (1981) bibliography of more than thirty sources.

Focus-group interviews, prevalent in market research, work best when an external consultant facilitates the process, but previous relationships with the facilitator may keep participants from being open or honest and may sidetrack discussion. Focus-group interviews, in addition to their inherent importance as data-gathering vehicles, have crucial importance as tools for preparing outcomes questionnaires or other instruments and for critiquing early drafts of such instruments. It is desirable to tape the proceedings for later coding and analysis, and for this two group facilitators can be helpful, especially in large groups. At certain points in the interview, it may be desirable for participants to break up into two- or three-person buzz groups, or to have group participants perform consensus-rendering activities, such as card sorts. Handouts can be used to help focus the group's attention and stimulate reactions.

A final category of self-report methods includes the Critical Incident Techniques and Behavioral Events Analysis. The former is actually a checklist (Knapp and Sharon, 1975). Students identify the extent of their own growth in knowledge, understanding, competence, skills, and values, or in other development. They then relate growth or lack of growth to what they perceive as critical factors contributing to or preventing desired growth. Those factors may be attitudes, environmental conditions or events, other individuals or groups, procedures and policies, or politics. Anecdotal records are often a part of the Critical Incident Technique.

Behavioral Events Analysis (McClelland, 1978; Pottinger and Klemp, 1976), developed at McBer and Company in Boston, is marketed by the Council for Adult and Experiential Learning. This one-to-one interview, which lasts two and a half hours, assesses student development in a variety of areas. In many respects, it is an expanded and refined version of the Critical Incident Technique. Successful as well as unsuccessful students are asked to identify and describe, in concrete and generic behavioral terms, events that they believe to have caused specified positive and negative outcomes and to tell all they know about these episodes, including their own feelings before, during, and after the events. Behavioral Events Analysis exploits people's tendency to remember most clearly episodes in which they are successful or overcome adversity.

Consensus-Rendering Techniques. Consensus among diverse people (such as students, their teachers, and observing experts) on whether a desired outcome has occurred, what its extent was, and why it occurred should lead to better understanding of that outcome. Consensus-rendering techniques are separate from the measures discussed previously. They include debates, juries, leaderless group discussions, hearings, concerns conferences, and reverse-flow conferences (Knapp and Sharon, 1975), as well as staffing conferences (Kelly and Dowd, 1975). Also included are card sorts and various modifications of the focus Delphi technique (Weaver, 1971). The Delphi technique is an iterative process of continuing to feed survey results back to respondents, after which respondents are once again surveyed. This procedure is generally repeated a set number of times, or until repeating the cycle yields little if any increase in group consensus. In the later stages, respondents whose estimates fall outside the interquartile range are often asked to justify their positions.

An "intelligence system" (Kotler, 1975) for assessing student outcomes consists of organizing and utilizing the entire network of people, inside and outside the institution, who come into contact with or hear about the institution's students. These people report to designated others to relay their observations. Some techniques that Kotler proposes are common in law enforcement, military intelligence, and weather forecasting but are seldom used in higher education.

Charette (Witkin, 1975) is a method of forcing agreement or consensus. It has been used extensively in the Kansas City Metropolitan Community College District but has received little attention or formal use elsewhere. It may appear informally near the end of a meeting, without the participants' even realizing that it is a technique. Charette consists of keeping the participants in the meeting room until an agreement (for example, about outcomes) acceptable to all is reached. In some ways, it is similar to the final phases of negotiation between a company and its workers' union.

Inventories. Another very common noncognitive data-gathering method is the inventory, a psychometric instrument that uses multiple-item or single-item scales to indicate characteristics of people or organizations. Inventories are generally written, but they can be oral and may involve manipulation of objects or (especially in occupational and vocational areas) perceptual exercises and activities. Some inventories employ self-reporting, while others subtly gather data without the subject's awareness. Some are subjective and projective, related to theoretical formulations, while others are objective and empirically derived.

Published standardized inventories have available reliability and validity coefficients, unless they are experimental and relatively untested. It is important to pay attention to the population on which norms for the instrument were based. For example, an instrument with norms based on traditional-age college students may be inappropriate for older students. Content and face validity are especially important, but other types of validity are important as well.

The *Ninth Mental Measurements Yearbook* (Mitchell, 1985), as well as the eight earlier ones by Buros, provide critical reviews invaluable for helping prospective users evaluate the quality and relevance of inventories in a wide range of areas. In addition, regular reviews of new inventories and other psychometric instruments, or new editions of established instruments, regularly appear in such journals as *Educational and Psychological Measurement, Measurement and Evaluation in Guidance,* and *Measurement in Education.* Bess (1979) has related a variety of commonly used inventories to different decision-making purposes. Hood (1986) describes and gives a brief history of inventories designed to measure Chickering's seven vectors of college student development. Mines (1982) has compiled a comprehensive list of instruments that purport to measure student development.

Criterion-referenced instruments are especially valuable noncognitive measures, and many of the scales presented in the sources already cited are of this type. Gronlund's (1973) and Berk's (1980, 1985) books on developing criterion-referenced measures can be helpful in developing one's own instruments or modifying any of those presented in the sources already cited. Other helpful books on applying and using noncognitive assessment data are Ewell (1984), Herman (1987), Lenning (1980), and

Lincoln and Guba (1985). Several national resource centers are available to help colleges and universities identify, develop, understand, and use noncognitive measures of educational outcomes.

Simulations. These are akin to performance measures, but they are distinctive because their design is especially crucial. Their implementation is entirely in the instructor's hands, and subtle discrepancies can cause the effort to fail. Like performance measures, simulation is designed to affect learning and be used simultaneously for assessment; learning and assessment receive equal emphasis and complement each other. The most common simulation method is role playing. Another prevalent method, highly visible as the primary curricular activity at the Harvard Business School, is the case study. Case studies, manipulated on computers, are becoming increasingly common. The dilemma-analysis exercise is a simulation method popular in philosophy courses and others across the curriculum that focus on ethics and values. Simulation games, used both for teaching and for outcomes assessment, are increasingly accessed by means of interactive computers. Other simulations are in-basket techniques (Knapp and Sharon, 1975) and logical-network analysis (Witkin, 1975).

Secondary Data Applications. Every institution collects data for accreditation, planning, budgeting, admissions, and grading. Some of these data may also have value for outcomes assessment. Grades and entrance test scores can be used to make judgments about grading practices and learning. Secondary data should never be primary indicators, however, but should be used only to supplement and clarify interpretations of the results obtained from primary indicators. Boyd and Westfall (1972) have developed criteria and procedures for determining when secondary data have sufficient validity and relevance to be used, and they discuss cautions and pitfalls associated with using them.

An indirect use of secondary data is the unobtrusive measure. For example, if visits to the campus art gallery increase significantly the year after a special series of lectures on art appreciation, then the lectures have probably had the desired impact. Library book use is another commonly used unobtrusive measure. Webb and others (1966) proposed a five-category typology of potential unobtrusive measures for colleges and universities to consider: physical traces (accretion and erosion); archival records; private records; simple observations; and contrived observations. Creative thinking is a key to developing unobtrusive measures, and Secrest (1973, 1979) has suggested that stimulative taxonomies may help us develop it.

Unusual Noncognitive Measures of Educational Outcomes

Each of the six broad categories of noncognitive measures discussed in the preceding section contains some unusual applications. For example, in performance measures, many written curriculum-embedded performances are uncommon, such as having all students in an English program teach writing to other college students, or having students live for four weeks in a utopian environment of their own design and read utopian literature (Student Learning Outcomes Task Force, 1980, pp. 15, 43). Fong's (1987) use of external examiners in assessment is also unique. Another example is interaction analysis (Amidon and Flanders, 1971), which records and analyzes interactions in the classroom; it now features computerized versions for recording data.

Cross's (1986) situation-specific classroom research is a new assessment concept, and innovative new models are appearing in business and industry, such as neurolinguistic programming and eye-assessing movements (Hart, 1986).

Noncognitive Measures for Cognitive and Noncognitive Outcomes

Since the early 1970s, Alverno College has developed and refined a sophisticated and effective assessment system that has gained national attention. Assessment focuses on eight different kinds of competence, each of which has six levels. Specific multiple measures have been formulated for each of these forty-eight levels, and data are continually gathered for each measure at the course, program, and institutional levels. Six of the eight kinds of competence are noncognitive: communication skills; making value judgments and independent decisions; social interaction; understanding the relationship of the individual to the environment; awareness and understanding of the world in which one lives; and knowledge, understanding, and responsiveness in the arts and humanities. Even for the remaining two kinds of competence, which are solely cognitive, noncognitive measures have been developed. Although the Alverno system as a whole is too complex and expensive for most colleges and universities, specific techniques and measures can be modified for new settings.

Pitfalls, Costs, and Benefits

Few would dispute the premise that the following noncognitive outcomes for college undergraduate education are important:

- Appreciation of the arts, history, and literature, and recognition of their ability to enhance insight into one's life
- Development of curiosity and fascination
- Ability to adjust to teaching styles that are not congruent with one's learning style
- Development of persistence, tolerance, understanding, and self-esteem

- Respect for other viewpoints and other persons
- Development of self-discipline in terms of effort, punctuality, and organization
- Ability to communicate and listen more effectively
- Ability to have good relations with others and to lead effectively
- A development of well-thought-out values and a philosophy of life.

In such noncognitive areas, at least, the array of possible outcome choices is not nearly so extensive as in cognitive knowledge areas, and Ewell (1985) has identified this discrepancy as a primary problem for institutions that wish to establish outcomes assessment programs: "What should students be expected to know by graduation? Much of the difficulty in establishing assessment programs is the general lack of agreement to this question" (p. 33). Even when noncognitive areas are well defined, however, people mean different things when they use such terms as *values, attitudes, understanding, appreciation, motivation,* and *perception.* Further, one still has to choose from an array of potential samples of the outcome. For example, appreciation, curiosity, and persistence can be used as criteria in any course or subject matter. One must choose representative behaviors or observations that indicate the presence of the desired educational outcome; which ones are chosen matters little, so long as they represent the outcome of concern. The important consideration is not the particular examples that are chosen; rather, what matters most is that decisions be made and pertinent data be collected and analyzed.

If the goals are specific and concrete enough for everyone to understand what is meant by the term *desired student outcomes,* deciding on measures becomes relatively easy. In higher education, however, goals are commonly not stated in concrete terms; they are only vaguely implied in process-oriented statements. This is probably the most significant and most common pitfall of using noncognitive measures of educational outcomes. Another is the complexity and the confounding that occur whenever multiple instruments are used to measure slightly different phenomena. It is easy to feel overwhelmed by the number and variety of noncognitive measures discussed in this chapter, but one must see this presentation for what it is: a broad "universe" from which to choose. Decide what should be measured, and then be selective.

Interviews have their own special pitfalls, including the difficulty of coding, analyzing, and interpreting data; the limited number of respondents; the difficulty of getting people to be interviewed and of obtaining representative samples of the population under study; and the subjectivity of the interviewer, which may introduce error. Berk (1986) lists the advantages and disadvantages of a number of other data-gathering methods.

Additional specific problems and pitfalls were referred to earlier, and there are others, including technical problems of validity and reliability, expense (in money and time), adverse effects on respondents' privacy, psychological impacts, defensiveness, and controversy. To some extent, however, such problems and pitfalls can be avoided and overcome, and many positive benefits, including funding, can be engendered.

Given the variety of available measures and the array of conditions and situations in which they can be used, it is impossible to generalize about the costs of noncognitive measures. As Ewell and Jones (1985) have pointed out, there are also "innumerable concepts of, and ways to calculate, costs . . . direct costs, indirect costs, full costs, average costs, marginal costs, and opportunity costs" (p. 34), to name a few. There are also the inconvenience and the psychological costs associated with planning, analysis, application, and coordination of noncognitive assessment procedures. Ewell and Jones (1985) cited costs of $29,201 for an assessment program at a liberal arts college of one thousand students ($8,175 for instruments, $713 for administering the instruments, and $20,313 for overhead and analysis), and costs of $130,084 at a major public university. According to Witkin (1984), as institutions move into the interactive mode, costs multiply (especially for one-to-one interviews) because of the time and money needed to train interviewers and group facilitators and the time needed to schedule and carry out separate interviews and code data before they are analyzed.

The reason why noncognitive measures are important even for cognitive outcomes is that inherent unreliability calls for multiple measures. Every measure has weaknesses; where one is weak, another may be strong. Multiple measures improve overall reliability and validity, without the excessive costs of designing a single instrument that would have the required degree of stability. Furthermore, in outcomes assessment one wants to observe change, and this project requires measures that are sensitive to change. Multiple measures show change without having adverse impacts on overall reliability.

Noncognitive measures can amplify understanding of how and why outcomes have occurred, and they allow several outcomes to be examined effectively at one time. Such measures are often more realistic, and they may be the only ones feasible for some hard-to-measure outcomes (Loveland, 1980). Finally, multiple measures enhance the effectiveness of student development transcripts, which some colleges have used to supplement academic transcripts and give prospective employers better insight into students' potential for success (Brown and Citrin, 1977).

References

Amidon, E. J., and Flanders, N. *A Manual for Understanding and Improving Teacher Classroom Behavior.* (Rev. ed.) St. Paul, Minn.: Association for Productive Teaching, 1971.

Bard, L. L. *Using Self-Reports to Predict Student Performance.* Research Monograph no. 7. New York: The College Board, 1976.

Berdie, D. R., Anderson, J. F., and Niebuhr, M. A. *Questionnaires: Design and Use.* (2d ed.) Metuchen, N. J.: Scarecrow Press, 1986.

Berk, R. A. (ed.). *Criterion-Referenced Measurement: State of the Art.* Baltimore, Md.: Johns Hopkins University Press, 1980.

Berk, R. A. (ed.). *A Guide to Criterion-Referenced Test Construction.* Baltimore, Md.: Johns Hopkins University Press, 1985.

Berk, R. A. (ed.). *Performance Assessment: Methods and Applications.* Baltimore, Md.: Johns Hopkins University Press, 1986.

Bess, J. L. "Classroom and Management Decisions Using Student Data." *Journal of Higher Education,* 1979, *50* (3), 256–279.

Boyd, H. W., and Westfall, R. *Marketing Research.* (3d ed.) Homewood, Ill.: Irwin, 1972.

Brown, R. D., and Citrin, R. S. "A Student Development Transcript: Assumptions, Uses and Formats." *Journal of College Student Personnel,* 1977, *18,* 163–168.

Cross, K. P. "Using Assessment to Improve Instruction." In *1986 Invitational Conference Proceedings: Assessing the Outcomes of Higher Education.* Princeton, N.J.: Educational Testing Service, 1986.

Edwards, A. L. *Techniques of Attitude Scale Construction.* East Norwalk, Conn.: Appleton-Century-Crofts, 1957.

Ewell, P. T. *The Self-Regarding Institution: Information for Excellence.* Boulder, Colo.: National Center for Higher Education Management Systems, 1984.

Ewell, P. T. (ed.). *Assessing Educational Outcomes.* New Directions for Institutional Research, no. 47. San Francisco: Jossey-Bass, 1985.

Ewell, P. T., and Jones, D. P. "The Costs of Assessment." In C. Adelman (ed.), *Assessment in American Higher Education: Issues and Contexts.* Washington, D.C.: Office of Educational Research and Improvement, U.S. Department of Education, 1985.

Fine, S. A. "Job Analysis." In R. A. Berk (ed.), *Performance Assessment: Methods and Applications.* Baltimore, Md.: Johns Hopkins University Press, 1986.

Fong, B. "The External Examiner Approach to Assessment." Paper presented to the American Association for Higher Education at the second National Conference on Assessment in Higher Education, Denver, June 14–17, 1987.

Gronlund, N. E. *Preparing Criterion-Referenced Tests for Classroom Instruction.* New York: Macmillan, 1973.

Guba, E. G., and Lincoln, Y. S. *Effective Evaluation: Improving the Usefulness of Evaluation Results Through Responsive and Naturalistic Approaches.* San Francisco: Jossey-Bass, 1981.

Hart, D. B. "Neurolinguistic Programming: An Innovative Approach to Effective Training in Industry." Paper presented at the Empire State College/State University of New York Conference on Value-Added Learning: New Strategies for Excellence in Education and Training, Saratoga Springs, N.Y., June 6, 1986.

Herman, J. L. (ed.). *Program Evaluation Kit.* (2d ed.) Newbury Park, Calif.: Sage, 1987.

Hood, A. B. *The Iowa Student Development Inventories.* Iowa City, Iowa: Hitech Press, 1986.

Kelly, F. D., and Dowd, E. T. "The Staffing Conference: An Approach to Student Evaluation." *Counselor Education and Supervision,* 1975, *15,* 135–139.

Knapp, J., and Sharon, A. *A Compendium of Assessment Techniques.* Princeton, N.J.: Educational Testing Service, 1975.

Kotler, P. *Marketing for Nonprofit Organizations.* Englewood Cliffs, N.J.: Prentice-Hall, 1975.

Lenning, O. T. *Previous Attempts to Structure Educational Outcomes and Outcome-Related Concepts: A Compilation and Review of the Literature.* Boulder, Colo.: National Center for Higher Education Management Systems, 1977.

Lenning, O. T. "Assessment and Evaluation." In U. Delworth and G. R. Hanson (eds.), *Student Services: A Handbook for the Profession.* San Francisco: Jossey-Bass, 1980.

Lincoln, Y. S., and Guba, E. G. *Naturalistic Inquiry.* Newbury Park, Calif.: Sage, 1985.

Loveland, E. (ed.). *Measuring the Hard-to-Measure.* New Directions for Program Evaluation, no. 6. San Francisco: Jossey-Bass, 1980.

McClelland, D. *Behavioral Events Interview.* Boston: McBer and Company, 1978.

Mines, R. A. "Student Development Assessment Techniques." In G. R. Hanson (ed.), *Measuring Student Development.* New Directions for Student Services, no. 20. San Francisco: Jossey-Bass, 1982.

Mitchell, J. V., Jr. (ed.). *The Ninth Mental Measurements Yearbook.* (2 vols.) Lincoln: University of Nebraska Press, 1985.

Oppenheim, A. N. *Questionnaire Design and Attitude Measurement.* New York: Basic Books, 1966.

Payne, S. L. *The Art of Asking Questions.* Vol. 3: Studies in Public Opinion. Princeton, N.J.: Princeton University Press, 1951.

Pottinger, P. S., and Klemp, G. O. *Concepts and Issues Related to the Identification, Measurement, and Validation of Competence.* Boston: McBer and Company, 1976.

Secrest, L. "Use of Innocuous and Noninterventional Measures in Evaluation." In B. R. Worthen and J. R. Sanders (eds.), *Educational Evaluation: Theory and Practice.* Worthington, Ohio: Jones, 1973.

Secrest, L. (ed.). *Unobtrusive Measurement Today.* New Directions for Methodology of Social and Behavioral Science, no. 1. San Francisco: Jossey-Bass, 1979.

Student Learning Outcomes Task Force. *Outcomes: Curriculum-Embedded Performances.* Washington, D.C.: Council of Independent Colleges, 1980.

Sudman, S., and Bradburn, N. M. *Asking Questions: A Practical Guide to Questionnaire Design.* San Francisco: Jossey-Bass, 1982.

Weaver, W. T. "The Delphi Forecasting Method." *Phi Delta Kappan,* 1971, 52 (5), 267–271.

Webb, E. J., Campbell, D. T., Schwartz, R. D., and Secrest, L. *Unobtrusive Measures: Nonreactive Research in the Social Sciences.* Skokie, Ill.: Rand McNally, 1966.

Whitney, D. R. *The Questionnaire as a Data Source.* University Examination Service, Technical Bulletin no. 13. Iowa City: The University of Iowa, 1972.

Witkin, B. R. *An Analysis of Needs Assessment Techniques for Educational Planning at State, Intermediate and District Levels.* Hayward, Calif.: Office of the Alameda County Superintendent of Schools, 1975.

Witkin, B. R. *Assessing Needs in Educational and Social Programs: Using Information to Make Decisions, Set Priorities, and Allocate Resources.* San Francisco: Jossey-Bass, 1984.

Oscar T. Lenning has been vice-president for academic affairs and academic dean at Roberts Wesleyan College in Rochester, New York. He will soon take office as executive vice-president and dean for academic affairs at Waldorf College in Forest City, Iowa. He was previously a senior associate at the National Center for Higher Education Management Systems and assistant director, Research Services Department, at the American College Testing Program.

Assessing the value added in education is a complex process that requires a careful research design and an understanding of the complex issues that affect how, when, and in what manner students are influenced by the education they receive.

Critical Issues in the Assessment of Value Added in Education

Gary R. Hanson

To examine how educational outcomes are attained, educational researchers must understand the assumptions that form the foundation of value-added models. To design good research, we must be aware of inherent pitfalls. Most of these problems are related to conceptual issues, psychometric questions, or research designs. A careful analysis of these three areas will show the importance of strategies that can explain how and why education adds value as students progress through college.

Underlying Assumptions in the Assessment of Value Added

The distinction between assessing student outcomes and assessing the value added by particular educational interventions seems clear. The focus of student outcomes assessment is on the "what" of education, and the focus of value added is on the "how." The assessment of value added forces a focus on the process of how educational goals are attained. Pascarella (1986) has defined the process of studying change and its antecedents as the "net effects" issue: "What kinds of students change in what kinds of ways when exposed to what kinds of educational experiences?"

T. W. Banta (ed.). *Implementing Outcomes Assessment: Promise and Perils.*
New Directions for Institutional Research, no. 59. San Francisco: Jossey-Bass, Fall 1988.

If we adopt this definition, we can assume the following assumptions: (1) that meaningful characteristics of students can be measured; (2) that both the nature and the magnitude of change in these characteristics can be assessed; and (3) that such change can be attributed to specific educational interventions. Assessing value added is a process that occurs over time; assessing when and how students change, and linking such change to specific educational interventions, is a complex and difficult task that requires new strategies for conceptualizing issues, building new and different assessment instruments, and designing research with different purposes and outcomes than those found in many traditional methods of inquiry.

Conceptual Issues

To assess how students change during college, we must think about the nature of student growth and development. Conceptual models and theories of student behavior are most useful when they help us focus on which student characteristics we should measure, when they should be measured, and how they change over time, as well as on the level of assessment specificity (global versus conditional) and the anticipated consequences (direct or indirect effects) of educational interventions. Ideally, theory and practical experience should be used in the planning stages of any assessment project to ensure that these important questions are considered.

What Should Be Measured? Answers to this question come from three primary sources: national and state reports on the condition of higher education, existing research literature, and theories of learning and psychological development. A few brief examples of information from these sources will illustrate the kinds and scope of the student characteristics that seem important to measure.

The Association of American Colleges (1985) lists four categories of essential student abilities: inquiry; abstract, logical thinking; critical analysis; and reading, writing, and speaking with distinction. An understanding of science, history, politics, the arts, and foreign cultures were other important learning requirements cited in the report.

Literature reviews, such as those developed by Bok (1986), Bowen (1977), and Pace (1979), not only recommend what has been systematically studied in the past but also provide insight into student characteristics that show some potential for change. Pace (1979), for example, lists eighteen college objectives that students accomplished as a result of attending college.

Most theories of learning and psychological development focus narrowly on certain dimensions of student characteristics, but what these theories lack in breadth they make up in rich conceptual detail. Knefel-

Figure 1. Critical Issues in the Assessment of Value Added in Education

The Change in Characteristic "X" for Three Students Over Four Years of College

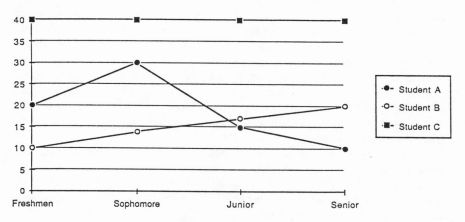

kamp, Widick, and Parker (1978) and Rodgers (1980) provide an overview of several popular theories about the cognitive, psychosocial, and moral development of students, while Gilligan (1982) and Kitchener (1982) offer interesting new theories for constructing assessments.

When Should Students Be Assessed? Another crucial issue in conceptualizing value-added research is appropriate timing for data collection. Traditionally, value-added research has focused on the changes that occur between the freshman and senior years, but such a strategy may miss important changes that occur in the sophomore and junior years. If data were collected each year on student characteristic X, results (shown in Figure 1) might show that three students had changed in very different ways, while collecting data only for the freshman and senior years would show no change. In Figure 1, the mean for the three students is the same in the senior year as in the freshman year. A conclusion of no change would be very misleading however, since student A shows a substantial gain in X from the freshman to the sophomore year but then loses that gain during the junior and senior years. This pattern is not at all unusual in students who take mathematics early in their college careers. Student B shows a gradual year-to-year gain, and student C shows a high performance in the freshman year, maintained for all four years. Students who already write well when they enter college may show this latter pattern. Hence, the timing of assessment is crucial. Theories of student learning and psychological development can help us know when to conduct assessment. Our knowledge about student learning patterns and other growth over the college years is equally important in the design of value-added assessment research.

How Do Student Characteristics Change Over Time? Knowing

not only when student characteristics change but also how they change is crucial. The design of instruments and research strategies requires an understanding of whether the quality of a characteristic changes as students learn. Again, theories may help us understand the nature of such change. Perry (1970) postulates that the quality of cognitive development changes in some predictable ways as students move from simple to more complex thought processes. Likewise, theories that include the suggestion that students move through a series of stages in their development often note qualitatively different aspects at each stage (Chickering, 1969; Erikson, 1968; Kohlberg, 1972; Perry, 1970). Other theorists—for example, Gilligan (1982)—suggest that students show gender-based qualitative differences in development.

Are the Effects of College on Students Global or Specific? In the conceptualizing of value-added assessment, a decision must be made about the level at which assessment is conducted (Pascarella, 1986). Traditionally, we have assumed that the influence of college on students is the same for all students—that is, that college has a global effect. This assumption ignores individual differences among students who attend the same institution or participate in the same educational activities. Students with different backgrounds or learning styles or levels of motivation may experience the same educational programs in dramatically different ways. Thus, college may be seen to produce conditional rather than general effects. If a value-added assessment is based on the assumption of general effects, conditional effects may be overlooked. The danger of assuming general effects is that a given educational intervention may show no influence over a large group of students, while for a particular subgroup the intervention is highly successful. If this issue is not considered at the stage of conceptualizing a value-added assessment, the research design may be inappropriate, and statistical analyses may fail to detect a change that has occurred.

Does College Influence Students Directly or Indirectly? To determine whether a given educational experience adds value to what students already know, it may be necessary to examine direct as well as indirect effects of experience on students. Limiting exploration to direct effects may exclude important and powerful effects that influence students indirectly. Pascarella, Terenzini, and Wolfle (1986) have shown that students exposed to freshman orientation before enrollment may experience few direct influences on first-year persistence, but that indirect effects of the orientation program may be overlooked if only direct effects are analyzed.

Implications. An effective value-added assessment project must consider all these conceptual issues. Ideally an assessment model should specify what characteristics will be measured, how they are likely to change over time, and when assessment will be conducted. The model must also indicate whether educational interventions are likely to influ-

ence all students in the same manner or affect subgroups of students in different ways. Finally, the model should specify how interventions will influence students. Will an educational program influence students directly, or indirectly through some other program? If researchers consider these questions and design a model of what is expected, they can avoid serious errors in interpretation once the data are analyzed.

Psychometric Questions

The psychometric and statistical problems of assessing changes in student development and learning have plagued educational researchers for a long time. Since many of the major issues have been summarized by others (Bereiter, 1963; Cronbach and Furby, 1970; Harris, 1963; Linn, 1981; and Pascarella, 1987), only a brief overview will be provided in this section. These problems are twofold: First, the psychometric characteristics of tests make the assessment of change difficult or impossible; and, second, the advantages and disadvantages of various statistical techniques for analyzing change in student characteristics are often not well understood. Nevertheless, new psychometric and statistical procedures have been developed to avoid some of these problems. A brief presentation of their applications is included in the following discussion.

Psychometric Problems of Assessing Change. One of the most serious psychometric problems associated with assessing changes in student characteristics is that most available assessment instruments were designed to measure static traits, rather than developmental changes (Hanson, 1982; Mines, 1985). Assessment instruments that measure static traits typically have high degrees of stability; that is, highly similar scores are obtained by students over time. In addition, most measures of static traits assume that the underlying structure of the construct being measured does not change with time. Hence, these assessment instruments may not detect student characteristics that change.

One reason such assessment instruments do not work well when measuring change is a result of the inverse relationship between stability and change-score reliability estimates. Linn (1981) shows how the reliability of change scores varies with levels of correlation between pre- and postmeasures when a static instrument is used. To the extent that an assessment instrument is a static test and there is a high correlation across two points in time, there will be lower reliability of the change scores for individuals. A low change-score reliability means that the measures are not capable of providing enough precision to allow accurate statements about individual change, although some careful statements about group change may still be possible. Another aspect of this issue is that when change-score reliability improves, test stability declines. Thus, the underlying structure of the measures is called into question. It is

difficult to have high change-score reliability without questioning whether a change in what is being measured has occurred.

Still another psychometric problem is that observed change is negatively correlated with initial testing status, and this relationship is a statistical artifact of measurement error (Bereiter, 1963). When the variance is approximately the same for the same measure taken at two different points in time, the correlation of the difference score with the first measure must be negative, by definition. Hence, in comparison of two groups over time, with existing first-time differences measured, the group that scores lower automatically shows greater change when measured the second time. This change has nothing to do with developmental growth or learning; again, it is an artifact of the measurement process.

Statistical Approaches to Analyzing Changes in Student Characteristics. Analyzing how students change, and attributing that change to educational interventions, has been studied and debated for years. Pascarella (1987) provides a comprehensive discussion of the advantages and disadvantages of most of the common statistical techniques. Only a brief overview will be presented here, with the recommendation that the interested reader review Pascarella for additional details.

Traditionally, the influence of an educational program on students has been studied by the assessment of students at some time before the intervention and again at some point afterward. The difference in the two scores was used as a measure of students' growth or learning. The difference in scores did provide a simple interpretation of the magnitude of change, but the difference scores were notoriously unreliable and were negatively correlated with students' initial status on the measure. Statisticians and psychometricians have warned against using simple pretest-to-posttest gain scores for years (Lord, 1967; Linn, 1981; Banta and others, 1987), but their warnings seem to have had slight impact on applied research.

An early approach to avoiding the problems associated with simple gain scores was the use of residual gain scores. This statistical procedure requires student outcome measures to be regressed on the input measures, so that a "predicted" outcome measure can be computed. The predicted outcome is then subtracted from the observed outcome and used as a measure of change. This residual score can be correlated with measures of the educational intervention to obtain a "part" correlation, which represents the unique association of the intervention with the outcome measure and eliminates the contribution of the input or original measure from the time when the first score was obtained. This residual gain score has the advantage of not being correlated with initial status, but it has the disadvantage of displaying a score metric that is different from the original. This difference leads to problems in interpretation. Moreover, the use of residual gain scores is limited to two-wave data, but

important changes may occur between the first and second measurements and may be overlooked. Another disadvantage of using the residual gain score to obtain the "part" correlation is the removal of any variance in the outcome measure that could be jointly attributable to the influence of both the input measure and the educational intervention. Hence, the residual score may overestimate the contribution of the input variable and underestimate that of the intervention. The bias introduced by this technique can be severe when there is a high correlation between the input measure and the intervention or a high correlation between the input and outcome measures.

Multiple correlation and regression analyses also have been used in the statistical analysis of change. Not only do these techniques provide a level of statistical control equal to that of residual scores and part or partial correlations, they also permit partition of the total variance of the dependent variables and an estimate of the relative influence of each independent variable on the dependent variable. The value of using a regression analysis is that it allows the researcher to estimate the net change in the outcome measure associated with unit changes in each of the independent variables. Nevertheless, the method does not help us understand how joint or common variance among independent variables may interact to influence outcome or dependent measures.

Causal analysis, sometimes referred to as path analysis, is a special application of regression analysis, which helps explain indirect as well as direct influences of independent variables on dependent variables. Its purpose is to determine the extent to which a preexisting model or set of interrelationships among variables is supported by actual data. Thus, models may be specified that include student background data, measures of educational intervention, and repeated measures of student growth and learning. Data are collected, and the pattern of relationships is tested to see if the data support the proposed model. While regression coefficients do not prove that causal relationships exist in the data, they may support the hypothesis that an observed relationship is causal. If the data do not support the model, then causal relationships can be disconfirmed (Pascarella, 1987; Wolfle, 1985). One advantage of causal analysis is that it forces the user to devise a model of the expected relationships among possible variables of interest. Not only must the independent and dependent variables be identified, the patterns of cause and effect among them must also be specified. Another advantage is that causal models allow researchers to examine direct as well as indirect effects—that is, some effects may not influence the dependent variable in a direct fashion but may influence one of the other variables in the model, which then may influence the dependent variable. To return to an example cited earlier (Pascarella, Terenzini, and Wolfle, 1986), an orientation program influenced the level of students' social integration into a college, and this

effect in turn influenced student persistence. This is one case in which causal analysis will detect the effect, while simple regression analysis will overlook it.

Causal analysis is not without its problems, however, and the most difficult one is to develop a sound model. If important variables of influence are excluded, the result is a biased model, with potentially inflated path coefficients suggesting stronger relationships among variables in the model than may actually exist. A second issue, identified by Pascarella (1987) and others, is recursiveness: Most causal models assume a unidirectional causal flow and the absence of any feedback influence, but most educational interventions may be better described as interactive, with multiple opportunities for feedback to influence the direction of the causal relationship. For example, does interaction with a faculty member after class improve a student's performance in the class, or do students who perform well in the class seek out the instructor after class? Testing which of the two possible causal links is supported by the data may require the collection of longitudinal data. If the variables are assessed in a cross-sectional study, there may be no way to determine whether a unidirectional cause-and-effect relationship exists. This problem can be overcome by use of a two-stage regression analysis and development of a nonrecursive causal model, but meeting the assumptions of this more complicated model are difficult, according to Wolfle (1985). Nevertheless, several recent studies have used this methodology to study student change in college (Bean and Bradley, 1986; Bean and Kuh, 1984; Iverson, Pascarella, and Terenzini, 1984). Measurement error is a third disadvantage cited by Pascarella. Causal modeling assumes that there is no measurement error, but this is rarely the case. When measurement error exists, the regression or path coefficients are biased in unknown ways, although the use of maximum-likelihood estimation procedures provides less biased estimates than other procedures do (Jöreskog and Sörbom, 1979).

Increasingly, researchers are calling for the use of multiwave data and more sophisticated models of student growth and development (Bryk and Weisberg, 1977; Bryk and Raudenbush, 1987; Strenio, Weisberg, and Bryk, 1983; Linn, 1981). The primary advantages of using growth curves based on multiple data points is that by plotting student changes, describing the nature of change, and noting the influence of educational interventions on subsequent measurement points, stronger statements can be made about the intervention's amount and type of influence.

One of the most promising statistical methods proposed for the study of change is the use of hierarchical linear models (Bryk and Raudenbush, 1987). This technique is based on regression analysis and can be used to study the structure of individual growth and the reliability of instruments for measuring status and change, assessing the correlates of status and change, and testing hypotheses about the effects of background

variables and educational interventions on individual growth. The use of this technique involves two stages of analysis. In the first stage, each individual's observed growth or development is considered as a function of an individual growth trajectory, plus random error. This growth trajectory is determined by use of a set of data points collected across time for each person. In the second stage, changes in the individual growth trajectory can be studied as functions of certain measurable characteristics of the individual's background (sex, age, ethnicity) and environment (participation in certain courses; extracurricular activities, or living arrangements).

The hierarchical linear model offers a number of statistical advantages over the use of other techniques. First, no assumptions are made about the nature of the growth curve. It need not be linear; it can be estimated on the basis of complex polynomial regression equations. Second, because the growth curve is estimated for each individual, this technique does not require the same data to be collected the same number of times for each individual. Thus, the problem of incomplete data, observed in longitudinal studies at various data-collection points, is simplified. Third, the variation in growth-curve models across individuals can be represented by a fixed between-subjects model, and changes in the growth parameters can be related to individuals' backgrounds or educational experiences. The between-subjects model can incorporate any number of background variables, and the between-subjects equation need not be identical for all growth parameters.

Hierarchical linear models provide flexibility in research design in that they allow a wide variety of between-subjects models and can be applied both to experimental and to quasi-experimental settings. This flexibility encourages researchers to expand the possible conceptualizations of research designs and eliminates the assumption that a given educational intervention adds a constant increment (or "value") to each individual (this assumption involves the issue of global versus conditional effects, mentioned earlier). Individuals may benefit to varying degrees, and this statistical technique will detect the magnitude and nature of changes. The primary disadvantage of the technique is that it requires sophisticated computer software programs that are not yet widely available.

Research Design

Because the assessment of value added in education assumes that students change over time, that the change can be measured, and that contributing influences on the quality and nature of change can be attributed to specific educational interventions, the design of research studies to support or refute evidence for such change is a most complicated affair. Careful consideration must be given to the selection of appropriate samples, the choice between a longitudinal or cross-sectional design, the determination of appropriate intervals between data-collection points, and the selection of units of analysis. In addition to the conceptual issues that make research design difficult in value-added assessment, issues specific to design also exist.

Isolating the Influence of Educational Interventions on Student Development. Potential influences on student growth and development can be categorized three ways: as intentional educational interventions, as unintentional educational interventions, and as growth or change that occurs without any kind of intervention (often called *maturation*). The first category includes all the planned courses, programs, and activities that we hope will influence students to change in beneficial ways. The second category includes the happy accidents that contribute to learning: We rarely have control over them, typically do not plan for them, but by putting students together on college campuses we may create them. We usually take credit for them, whether or not they were intentional, and call them "college effects." The third category includes experiences that are likely to happen to all individuals of a particular age and that are unrelated to the educational setting. Forming relationships with other people, learning to live independently, and maturing physically are developmental tasks that everyone experiences, regardless of attendance at college. The rate at which these tasks are fulfilled and the quality of the experience may differ, but the influence of maturation may be difficult to separate from the college experience. One of the most critical problems in value-added research design is to isolate the relative contribution of each type of influence on the growth and learning that students experience while attending college.

One approach to isolating relative effects is to use a control sample of students, who are followed over the same period of time but are not allowed to participate in the educational intervention under study. Control groups are often difficult to locate, however: Community standards, ethical concerns, and legal issues surrounding the restriction of certain educational practices make it difficult to use adequate control groups in a research design; random exposure of students to educational opportunities is almost never an option. Pascarella (1986) has suggested combined cross-sectional and longitudinal research designs, or the use of returning adult students to constitute comparison groups, as alternative designs that take maturation into consideration. The difference between longitudinal and cross-sectional results, adjusted for the effects of selective attrition, might be used as an estimate of normal maturation during college.

Isolating the effects of unintentional educational interventions is undoubtedly much more difficult, because these can rarely be discerned

during data collection. Often, happy accidents come to light only when we try to explain some unusual finding. In monitoring the relative effects of multiple interventions, some degree of control is possible if we carefully document which students are participating in which of several possible educational activities (only some of which are the ones assessed intentionally). Students' involvement in extracurricular activities that lead to critical thinking, leadership skills, and social competence may well occur in a regular fashion outside the structured curriculum, and the preferred approach would be to identify the level of involvement and incorporate such variables as possible influences of growth and development into model building and research design. Obviously, the ethics of confidentiality and respect for individual rights would prohibit the monitoring of many unintentional educational interventions.

Choosing Appropriate Units of Analysis. Research designs used to study the effects of educational interventions on student growth and learning may use several units of analysis: the institution, classes or departments at a single institution, or the individual. For any given study, one unit of analysis may be more appropriate than another, but the use of different units of analysis forces a focus on different kinds of questions (Burstein, 1980; Pascarella, 1987). When the institution is the unit of analysis, the study results will answer questions about the average influence of the educational intervention on the average level of student development. Aggregating data at the institutional level tends to ignore possible variations among individual students' experiences within a single institution. When the individual is the unit of analysis, the focus is on whether differences in the individual's involvement in various educational activities lead to differences in specific outcomes; the data may be collected across multiple institutions, but the focus is still on the individual. Focusing on the individual, however, ignores other important questions, such as those that involve institutionwide influences on growth and learning. For example, the manner in which interaction with faculty facilitates student learning may be different at large and small institutions. A study that uses the individual as the unit of analysis and collects data across multiple institutions may miss this source of influence, even when controlling for differences in individual characteristics. Research studies that incorporate multiple levels of analysis (Burstein, 1980; Cronbach, 1976; Linn, 1981; Terenzini and Pascarella, 1984) avoid the problem of using only a single unit of analysis and thereby missing important influences on student development.

Choosing an Appropriate Number of Data-Collection Points. A design issue highly related to timing is the selection of an appropriate number of data-collection points. Both theory and experience help determine appropriate times to assess students. Timing is crucial to determining starting and ending points, but other factors often influence the number of possible data-collection points available in between. If the assessment is started either too early or too late, or if it ends at the wrong time, the opportunity to observe and assess change in student character-istics is missed. Assessment that includes only two data-collection points may actually capture the total amount of change but will provide too few data-collection points to answer important questions about when change occurred in the total time interval. In addition, important infor-mation about the nature of the change, as it unfolds, is lost.

General Principles for Assessing Value-Added Education

The purpose of this chapter has been to identify some issues that are crucial to conducting research whose goal is to assess if and how students change and, more important, what factors contribute to such change. The following principles can be used as guidelines for imple-menting future studies.

Principle 1: Decide whether the purpose of the study is to assess student outcomes, or value added from educational interventions. Assess-ment of student outcomes is descriptive and determines only how students appear at the end of a certain period. To assess value added by educa-tional intervention, one must focus on the process of how students change. Not only is the nature of change important to assess, but under-standing the causes of change is also necessary to determine whether value has been added. The research designs and statistical analyses required to pursue value-added assessments are different from those used for assessment of student outcomes.

Principle 2: Build a model to represent variables of interest and their relation to outcomes. Since determination of value added is a process and not just an outcome, diagramming is essential. Knowing what to measure and when, anticipating types of changes that may occur, and including measures of the interventions likely to influence changes are prerequisites both of good design and of effective data collection and analysis. Causal modeling and hierarchical linear regression require specification of how growth is likely to occur. It is impossible to design and conduct good research without appropriate models of what is expected to happen.

Principle 3: Identify or build instruments that assess both status and change. The psychometric instruments available to higher education have done an excellent job of measuring a student's status at a single point in time, and they have been most useful in telling us how one student differed from another. To measure change, however, the assessment instru-ment must be capable of telling us how an individual student changes over time; the comparison with other students is less important. Such instruments not only must assess the magnitude of change but also must detect qualitative differences in underlying dimensions that are subject to change as a result of an educational intervention. New formats and scoring procedures are needed to summarize these kinds of assessment instruments.

Principle 4: Use theory and practical experience to identify critical data-collection points. After experiencing different kinds of educational interventions, students change at different times and at different rates. Completing an assessment before change has occurred is a waste of time and money, and collecting data long after the influence of an educational intervention has dissipated is likewise unproductive. Collecting data too infrequently may allow an accurate assessment of the magnitude of a change but may also prevent observation of the qualitative nature of the change. Hence, one of the most critical aspects of conducting good value-added assessment is knowing when and how many times to collect data. Some educational theories may provide ideas of how students change. These can guide research design. Likewise, faculty and staff knowledge that comes from day-to-day interaction with students also provides a good framework for collecting data at the optimum times.

Principle 5: Use statistical techniques appropriate to the analysis of change. In spite of admonitions to the contrary, researchers continue to use simple gain scores, collected at two different times, to measure the amount of change in student characteristics. These gain scores are often correlated with measures of educational intervention to determine the degree of influence. Inappropriate and incorrect interpretations nearly always result. Building good models (see Principle 1), and using causal analysis and hierarchical linear models to analyze the resulting data, will permit more sophisticated interpretation of a change and its correlates. Using poor or inappropriate data-analysis techniques can only obscure what we learn about how students change as a result of educational experiences.

References

Association of American Colleges. *Integrity in the College Curriculum: A Report to the Academic Community.* Washington, D.C.: Association of American Colleges, 1985.

Banta, T., Lambert, W., Pike, G., Schmidhammer, J., and Schneider, J. "Estimated Student Score Gain on the ACT COMP Exam: Valid Tool for Institutional Assessment?" Paper presented at the annual meeting of the American Educational Research Association, Washington, D.C., April 1987.

Bean, J., and Bradley, R. "Untangling the Satisfaction-Performance Relationship for College Students." *Journal of Higher Education,* 1986, 57, 393–412.

Bean, J., and Kuh, G. "The Reciprocity Between Student-Faculty Informal Contact and the Undergraduate Grade Point Average of University Students." Paper presented at the annual meeting of the Association for the Study of Higher Education, Chicago, 1984.

Bereiter, C. "Some Persisting Dilemmas in the Measurement of Change." In

66

C. W. Harris (ed.), *Problems in the Measurement of Change*. Madison: University of Wisconsin Press, 1963.

Bok, D. *Higher Learning*. Cambridge, Mass.: Harvard University Press, 1986.

Bowen, H. R. *Investment in Learning: The Individual and Social Value of American Higher Education*. San Francisco: Jossey-Bass, 1977.

Bryk, A. S., and Raudenbush, S. W. "Application of Hierarchical Linear Models to Assessing Change." *Psychological Bulletin*, 1987, *101* (1).

Bryk, A. S., and Weisberg, H. I. "Use of Nonequivalent Control Group Design When Subjects are Growing." *Psychological Bulletin*, 1977, *84*, 950–962.

Burstein, L. "The Analysis of Multilevel Data in Educational Research and Evaluation." In D. Berlinger (ed.), *Review of Research in Education*. Vol. 8. Washington, D.C.: American Educational Research Association, 1980.

Chickering, A. *Education and Identity*. San Francisco: Jossey-Bass, 1969.

Cronbach, L. J. *Research on Classrooms and Schools: Formulation of Questions, Design, and Analysis*. Palo Alto, Calif.: Stanford Evaluation Consortium, Stanford University, 1976.

Cronbach, L. J., and Furby, L. "How We Should Measure Change—Or Should We?" *Psychological Bulletin*, 1970, *74*, 68–80.

Erikson, E. *Identity: Youth and Crisis*. New York: Norton, 1968.

Gilligan, C. *In a Different Voice*. Cambridge, Mass.: Harvard University Press, 1982.

Hanson, G. R. (ed.). *Measuring Student Development*. New Directions for Student Services, no. 20. San Francisco: Jossey-Bass, 1982.

Harris, C. *Problems in the Measurement of Change*. Madison: University of Wisconsin Press, 1963.

Iverson, B., Pascarella, E., and Terenzini, P. "Informal Faculty-Student Contact and Commuter College Freshmen." *Research in Higher Education*, 1984, *21*, 123–136.

Jöreskog, K., and Sörbom, D. *Advances in Factor Analysis and Structural Equation Models*. Cambridge, Mass.: Abt Books, 1979.

Kitchener, K. "Human Development and the College Campus: Sequences and Tasks." In G. R. Hanson (ed.), *Measuring Student Development*. New Directions for Student Services, no. 20. San Francisco: Jossey-Bass, 1982.

Knefelkamp, L., Widick, C., and Parker, C. (eds.). *Applying New Developmental Findings*. New Directions for Student Services, no. 4. San Francisco: Jossey-Bass, 1978.

Kohlberg, L. "Stages of Moral Development." In C. M. Beck, B. S. Crittenden, and E. V. Sullivan (eds.), *Moral Education*. Toronto: University of Toronto Press, 1972.

Linn, R. L. "Measuring Pretest-Posttest Performance Changes." In R. Berk (ed.), *Educational Evaluation Methodology: The State of the Art*. Baltimore, Md.: Johns Hopkins University Press, 1981.

Lord, F. "A Paradox in the Interpretation of Group Comparisons." *Psychological Bulletin*, 1967, *68*, 304–305.

Mines, R. A. "Measurement Issues in Evaluating Student Development Programs." *Journal of College Student Personnel*, 1985, *26* (2), 101–106.

Pace, C. R. *Measuring Outcomes of College: Fifty Years of Findings and Recommendations for the Future*. San Francisco: Jossey-Bass, 1979.

Pascarella, E. T. "Are Value-Added Analyses Valuable?" Paper presented at the annual Educational Testing Service Invitational Conference, New York, October 25, 1986.

Pascarella, E. T. "Some Methodological and Analytic Issues in Assessing the

Influence of College." Paper presented at joint meeting of the American College Personnel Association and the National Association of Student Personnel Administrators, Chicago, 1987.

Pascarella, E., Terenzini, P., and Wolfle, L. "Orientation to College and Freshman Year Persistence/Withdrawal Decisions." *Journal of Higher Education*, 1986, *57*, 155-175.

Perry, W., Jr. *Forms of Intellectual and Ethical Development in the College Years: A Scheme.* New York: Holt, Rinehart & Winston, 1970.

Rodgers, R. "Theories Underlying Student Development." In D. G. Creamer (ed.), *Student Development in Higher Education.* Cincinnati, Ohio: American College Personnel Association (ACPA) Media, 1980.

Strenio, J.L.F., Weisberg, H. I., and Bryk, A. S. "Empirical Bayes Estimation of Individual Growth Curves Parameters and Their Relationship to Covariates." *Biometrics*, 1983, *39*, 71-86.

Terenzini, P., and Pascarella, E. "Freshman Attention and the Residential Context." *Review of Higher Education*, 1984, *7*, 11-124.

Wolfle, L. "Applications of Causal Models in Higher Education." In J. Smart (ed.), *Higher Education: Handbook of Theory and Research.* New York: Agathon Press, 1985.

Gary R. Hanson is coordinator of research for the Office of Admissions at the University of Texas, Austin.

To determine whether we are getting our money's worth from assessment efforts in higher education, costs must be linked more fully and accurately with their informational outcomes.

Costs and Benefits of Assessment: A Paradigm

Darrell R. Lewis

Issues surrounding the need for more and better assessment in higher education have been raised increasingly at all levels of funding and concern. In fact, most recent discussion of these issues has focused almost exclusively on this need, with little attention to whether or how we can get our money's worth from such efforts. This chapter focuses on the development of a paradigm whereby assessment costs in higher education can be linked more fully and accurately with their informational outcomes. It is important to note at the outset that our unit of interest for determining costs and benefits is the assessment project itself, and not the inputs and outputs of the units or programs being assessed.

Evaluation activities in higher education have been justified on the basis of numerous expressed reasons and have promised certain desirable outcomes. The most commonly expressed rationale is the need for improving a program's or an institution's effectiveness: How well is the program meeting its stated goals, and what changes can we make to enhance the desirable outcomes? A second justification offered for assessment reflects the need for fiscal accountability, either to the institution or to external agencies: Have the funds been allocated and used for their intended purpose? A third and increasingly important rationale for assessment in higher education has been the need for improving decisions

T. W. Banta (ed.). *Implementing Outcomes Assessment: Promise and Perils.*
New Directions for Institutional Research, no. 59. San Francisco: Jossey-Bass, Fall 1988.

about program efficiency and resource allocation: How cost-effective is the program in meeting its stated goals? Obviously, all three of these rationales and their related questions are interconnected. Nevertheless, each addresses a separate issue and requires separate evaluation-design considerations. Equally important, each of these expressed needs and outcomes requires the use of resources and the imposition of costs on the project being evaluated. These latter costs are often forgotten or minimized when arguments are made for the benefits of more and better assessment information in higher education.

Limited Attention to Assessment Costs

Although some recent literature has begun to address the issues of assessment costs and benefits, as well as their interrelationships (Alkin and Ruskus, 1984; Alkin and Solmon, 1983; Catterall, 1983; Haggart, 1983; and Morell and Weirich, 1983), scant literature in higher education focuses on either the availability or the utility of such information for making institutional policies and decisions. A few studies from the past decade report on empirical cost data in higher education (Bowen, 1980; NACUBO, 1977; Verry and Davies, 1976), but only two, by Bowen (1985) and by Ewell and Jones (1985), address the costs of assessment, and then only in simulated case studies of estimating probable costs for selective types of testing, without linkage to valued outcomes. The higher education literature contains neither a single cost-effectiveness or cost-utility analysis of assessment nor any empirically based institutional case study of the costs of assessment (Conrad and Wilson, 1985).

With evaluation at all levels increasingly focused on effectiveness, accountability, and efficiency, it is clear that individual institutions are the primary locus of control for these matters. It is also clear that institutional policymakers and administrators need reliable and complete (total and average) cost information for initiating or replicating educational assessment projects. Furthermore, they need to know incremental (marginal) costs in order to make decisions about expanding or reducing assessment projects and service areas. They need to know what it costs to provide assessment for a particular activity or program. In higher education, the responsibility, data, and capacity for making such decisions are mainly at the institutional level.

The Value of Information in Assessment

Although largely ignored in the evaluation literature, work in economics that deals with the economics of information (Alchian and Demsetz, 1972; Hirschleifer, 1971; Stigler, 1961), as well as work in the management sciences that addresses the value of information to managerial decision making (Decision Analysis Group, 1976; Huber, 1980), does give a useful theoretical foundation and introductory paradigm for viewing the link between costs and benefits that results from assessment in higher education. For example, decision-tree and probability techniques are being used in a growing body of decision-theory literature to determine the net expected value that might result from a particular decision to seek information. All the known illustrations that use these techniques in the economics and management literature require costs as well as benefits to be expressed in dollars.

This conceptual framework, wherein benefits are defined in informational terms, also has been employed in the applied consumer-economics literature (Day, 1978). The need for such information seems essential to any number of decision-model approaches to evaluation (Popham, 1975), but only one source (Catterall, 1983) has used the information paradigm, and it was used in the context of public school testing. No one has systematically employed the framework in the context of higher education assessment.

The basic economic question that this literature addresses concerns the amount of resources that a decision maker should allocate in the search for information. This line of inquiry is clearly applicable to the concerns of this chapter. By its very nature, assessment in higher education seeks information to improve external accountability, internal effectiveness, or internal efficiency.

A Cost-Benefit Paradigm for Assessment

Basically, the usefulness of such evaluation information is its primary benefit in higher education assessment, and increased benefits can be obtained by designing assessment procedures that enhance the information's utility. These benefits (or the utility of the resulting information) must be weighed against the costs of each evaluation project in order to determine the information's cost benefit or cost utility. Each of these latter efficiency measures can then be compared in turn with similar measures for alternative assessment projects, or with the consequences of doing nothing, in order to determine their relative importance and priority. This typology of costs and benefits, with benefits expressed in informational terms, provides an appropriate goal set and overview for examining evaluation in higher education, as illustrated in Table 1.

Our paradigm of costs and benefits linked to informational outcomes suggests that the costs and benefits of alternative assessment projects in higher education can be conceived in equivalent terms (that is, their impact on a set of informational goals dealing with educational accountability, effectiveness, and efficiency). Moreover, optimal amounts of evaluation are, at least in theory, identifiable when combined with

Table 1. The Costs and Benefits of Assessment in Higher Education: Who Benefits and Who Bears the Burden?

Costs and Benefits of Evaluation	Perspectives			
Costs	Staff[a]	Institution[b]	Students[c]	Society[d]
Direct Resource Costs				
Personnel and Consultants		−		−
Facilities and Equipment		−		−
Supplies and Materials		−		−
Travel and Data Processing		−		−
Incidental and Opportunity Costs				
Possible Diminished Morale/ Collegiality	−	−	−	
Possible Legal and Moral Burdens	−	−		
Possible Misinformation		−	−	−
Opportunity Costs of Student Time			−	
Opportunity Costs of Staff Time	−	−		−
Opportunity Costs of Monitoring				−
Benefits				
Direct Information Benefits				
Improved Accountability	+/−	+/−	+	+
Improved Effectiveness	+	+	+	+
Improved Efficiency	+/−	+	+	+
Incidental and Secondary Benefits				
Incidental Student Learning			+	
Incidental Changes in Staff Attitudes	+/−	+/−	+/−	
Incidental Knowledge Production				+
New/Declined Accreditation	+/−	+/−	+/−	+
Increased/Decreased Quality Students	+/−	+/−	+/−	
Increased/Decreased External Resources	+/−	+/−	+/−	−/+

[a] Faculty and administration in program evaluated.
[b] Other institutional faculty and staff, including administration, overseers, and evaluators.
[c] Viewed as sole consumers of institutional product.
[d] Includes donors, government agencies, legislatures, foundations, parents, and alumni.

Source: Adapted from Lewis and Wasescha, 1987.

cost information. Further, selections of alternative assessment projects can be made rationally (that is, with benefit-cost comparisons). It is generally understood in the evaluation literature (Joint Committee on Standards for Educational Evaluation, 1981, p. 60) that when the costs of evaluation start to exceed its (informational) benefits, no further evaluation should be carried out. This formulation resembles Bowen's (1974) notion of cost effectiveness, Scriven's (1983) description of cost-free evaluation, and Catterall's (1983) typology of costs and benefits dealing with the optimal amount of testing in the public schools.

Cost Consequences of Assessment in Higher Education

In the employment of any evaluation design for assessment in higher education, additional resources are allocated for these purposes, and there are obviously cost consequences. Detailed information about the deployment of these resources and their costs in each evaluation project helps, first of all, to identify inefficiencies in resource use and to suggest needed improvements in the evaluation design for each individual project. Second, cost information aids in determining whether the assessment project is feasible, given whatever budget or cost constraints may exist in the program or the institution. Third, such cost information also contributes to a determination of whether an assessment project's overall value is worth the cost, when the information is linked to the project's overall outcome benefits. Fourth, cost information is essential for any type of cost-benefit or cost-utility comparison of alternative assessment projects.

To assess the cost consequences of assessment, one must first establish a manageable framework by which to assess the direct resource requirements for each evaluation, along with a method for translating these requirements into cost estimates. Next, one needs to assess the likely incidental and opportunity costs of the project, both to the institution and to society.

Direct Resource Components. The cost analysis recommended for determining the direct resource costs within this framework is conventionally known as a *resource components approach.* This approach requires the specification and measurement of all the specific resources employed for each evaluation project, and then the valuing and costing out of each resource to determine total costs for the project (see, for example, Chambers and Parrish, 1984; Levin, 1983). As desired, total costs can then be standardized or converted into per-unit costs for inter-project comparisons on the basis of any common institutional currency, such as the number of students, instructional hours, credits, or courses that the program or the institution offers.

Direct institutional resource costs, as well as other, nonbudgetary institutional costs, can and should be accounted for in the analysis. Total resource costs of assessment services and activities include not only direct expenditures, according to their ingredient or resource components (including fringe benefits to all personnel), but also travel costs; payments to external agencies, vendors, and consultants; imputed and annualized costs for facilities, equipment, and data processing; and other administrative costs. The actual accounting framework is not important; what is important is simply that all resources that may be used in the evaluation be identified, measured, and counted. Some useful sources that can assist the evaluator in identifying and valuing the prices of resources in higher education are Bowen (1980, 1985), Halstead (1975, with annual supplements through 1978), and the annual reports of the National Center for Educational Statistics.

Incidental and Opportunity Costs of Evaluation. A number of incidental and opportunity costs likely to result from assessment in higher education are identified in the accounting framework of Table 1. While some of these indirect and incidental costs have been noted by others (Alkin and Ruskus, 1984; Alkin and Solmon, 1983; and Catterall, 1983), many have been ignored in the evaluation literature, and there has been no systematic attempt to examine or measure them in the context of higher education.

Two possible consequences of evaluation in higher education are diminished collegiality and lessened productivity of institutional staff, resulting from real or perceived intrusions on academic or work freedoms (Seeley, 1981). Similarly, diminished staff morale may result from anticipation of either negative or unrealistically positive results (Armstrong, 1982).

In addition, the issues and legal requirements of openness ("sunshine laws") in public higher educational institutions also have implications for assessment costs. In states with such laws, it is quite apparent that all nonpersonnel assessment results are public information. In the context of higher education, Cleveland (1985) has examined these legal requirements and has concluded that they can often lead to some negative effects (costs), both to the institution and to society. He notes, for example, a loss of candor in individual responses to various forms of evaluation when anonymity is not ensured, and he observes that results of evaluation, if negative, are often reported in simplified and trivialized form. He also reports that openness generates administrative costs for reporting purposes and, at worst, may encourage criminal behavior (for example, by individuals who attempt to circumvent legal requirements).

Trow (1975) argues that the growing external concern for accountability, effectiveness, and efficiency in higher education "increases the role of nonacademic authorities in the decisions about what goes on in its institutions" (p. 116) and is "on balance most harmful" (p. 122). Informational results are often based either on misinformation or on measurement with a too-limited focus. Trow maintains that externally generated demands for evaluation cannot effectively measure and assess all the unique and long-term outcomes resulting from higher education. On balance, he says, such demands result in negative effects, especially for research universities. Alkin and Solmon (1983) also hold that when evaluation projects focus on rather narrow or immediately observable objectives, certain long-term goals may be slighted or even ignored altogether.

Student and faculty time taken from teaching and learning must also be accounted for as a real but intangible cost. The opportunity costs of staff time and use of facilities can and should be accounted for within direct costs whenever possible, but other possible opportunity costs to society should be recognized by decision makers. Catterall (1983) has noted, for example, the additional cost of the time that a state agency may spend legislating, developing, and monitoring evaluation.

How Much Should Evaluation Cost?

The preceding discussion has focused on cost feasibility: How much does a particular evaluation cost? There have been several attempts to estimate guidelines for how much an evaluation should cost in relation to the overall budget of an educational program, but these have not undertaken an actual review of resource components. Many granting agencies have insisted on evaluation of whatever projects or programs they may fund, and some have sought guidelines for funding this component. Similarly, administrative decision makers, program developers, and evaluation analysts have been concerned with how to budget for evaluation. Conventional wisdom has held that all one needed to do was empirically assess the model costs of evaluation and then use these results for planning and funding.

The results of these attempts have varied widely. Rusnell (1979, p. 97) reports that 10 percent of a program's cost "is sometimes suggested for use in evaluation," but he offers this guideline without rationale. The Minnesota State Department of Education has reported (Lewis and Wasescha, 1987) that some state guidelines for Title III and Title IV projects recommend from 4 percent to 6 percent of the overall budget for evaluation. Similarly, the results of a survey of public school evaluators by Drezek, Monkowski, and Higgins (1982) indicate that an evaluation budget of at least 4 to 8 percent is preferred. In higher education, Bowen, (1985, p. 18) has recommended that institutions devote between 1 percent and 3 percent of their educational budgets to evaluation and to related research and development. The Joint Committee on Standards for Educational Evaluation (1981, p. 187) recommends, without further rationale, that the evaluation budget constitute about 10 percent of total program or project budget.

In practice, however, Abrahamson and Wholey (1981) have found that most federally funded educational evaluations are supported largely by 1 percent setaside funds in the authorizing legislation. Others (Drezek, Monkowski, and Higgins, 1982; Webster and Stufflebeam, 1978) have found that in the public schools, less than one-third of 1 percent of total budgets is typically devoted to educational evaluation. There are no current federal guidelines or rules governing the size of evaluation budgets. From these surveys, all we now have are varying guidelines and estimates, ranging from less than 1 percent to over 10 percent. These guidelines have almost no rationale except (presumably) the availability of funds.

Alkin and Stecher (1983) have reported the results of an interview survey designed to determine whether factors such as type of evaluation being conducted (formative or summative) and total budget size affected the number and types of evaluation costs. Their study indicated that the cost of each evaluation was a highly variable and individual matter closely linked to the goals and design of the project. Morell and Weirich (1983) and Haggart (1983) similarly reported that the unique characteristics of each evaluation have important impacts on cost. Most impacts are rather obvious. As the number of units being evaluated increases, the total cost increases, while the cost per unit declines. Decisions regarding the complexity of the evaluation design, the level of data requirements, and the type of data collection and analysis all have obvious effects on the evaluation's resource requirements, and thus on its cost. As Alkin and Ruskus (1984, p. 12) have concluded, "our research on the costs of evaluation has convinced us that it is difficult, if not impossible, to generalize about the direct or indirect costs associated with evaluations of different types."

A recent telephone survey of large private foundations by Lewis and Wasescha (1987) indicates that the directors of such funding organizations are becoming much more knowledgeable about the needs and inherent costs of evaluation, and that they are no longer using or seeking numerical guidelines. Many of the directors reported that evaluation can "appropriately" cost anywhere from nothing to 100 percent of the program budget, as determined by evaluation objectives and design. In short, the real issue to these informed foundation leaders is neither the dollar cost of an evaluation nor the cost of the assessment project relative to the cost of the program being assessed; rather, it is the relationship between the costs and benefits resulting from the evaluation project itself. Today it is clear that many professional staffs of private funding agencies are conversant with evaluation costs and are developing at least intuitive perspectives on evaluation cost-benefit paradigms for planning and funding.

Benefits of Assessment in Higher Education

All the direct information benefits shown in the second part of Table 1 can be tied to the overall informational goals of evaluation in higher education, but evaluation also induces other incidental and secondary benefits. One is the incidental learning of students through the evaluation process itself. In addition, other actors in the evaluation process (for example, faculty, administrators, alumni, and employers) are likely to be indirectly affected by the process. Indirect benefits may include greater concern for and attention to what is being assessed, as a result of the evaluation process and specification of goals by faculty and administrators (Dornbusch, 1979). Another possible indirect benefit is more favorable external attitudes toward the program or institution, because of the actors' perceived importance in contributing to the process. Still another incidental benefit is assessment's potential contribution to knowledge (and to scholarly literature) and the use of that knowledge outside the institution.

Of course, the most important benefits of assessment in higher education are (1) the secondary effects and (2) the actual ways that external parties and agencies use the direct informational benefits. New or renewed accreditation may result; better and different students may enroll in greater numbers; and increased resources may come from students, foundations, donors, and legislatures. Recent research in consumer economics (Day, 1978, p. 137) clearly indicates that enhanced confidence and satisfaction are the principal outcomes of information disclosure in consumer affairs. It is reasonable to expect similar results from assessment in higher education. From the perspective of the society outside the institution, the secondary effects of information benefits may also be valuable and important if they lead to loss of accreditation, reduced enrollments, or decreased resources at particular institutions.

Benefits and Burdens of Assessment

The issue of perspective has often been overlooked in reviewing the costs and benefits of assessment. Perspective involves determining who gains the benefits and who bears the burden of costs. Detailed review of the various secondary costs and benefits of evaluation is beyond the scope of this chapter, but it is useful to consider their effects on the primary stakeholders in the assessment process, for only in the interests of these major groups does assessment information take on value or cost. For ease of illustration, the major stakeholders are grouped in Table 1 according to four major perspectives: staff of the program under review; other institutional staff, including administrators, evaluators, and overseers; students; and other interested individuals outside the institution.

First, and most important, students, as the primary consumers of the educational product, are the greatest stakeholders in its assessment. They share the burden of almost all the costs, and they benefit from almost all the outcomes. Second, benefits accrue to various stakeholders differentially, according to the results of the assessment. Third, the staff of the program being assessed does not have the same stake either in costs or in outcomes as the institution or other stakeholders do. For example, if the informational outcomes reflect negatively on the program under review, the program staff may lose status or resources, while the institu-

78

tion or other stakeholders may gain valuable information for decision making. Fourth, society shares directly and indirectly in the costs and benefits of assessment in higher education.

The cost-benefit paradigm described in this chapter for selecting among assessment projects is important, but by itself it will not substitute for administrative judgment. No one with any experience in higher education believes that true institutional assessment for accountability, effectiveness, or efficiency (or the selection of alternative projects for such purposes) can be achieved by gathering a few bits of data, feeding the data into a model, and reading off the answers. The process is bound to be difficult and, in the end, subjective and judgmental. Nevertheless, judgments concerning which projects to undertake can be better informed and made more credible by the systematic gathering of facts about costs and benefits and by analyses like the one described in this chapter.

References

Abrahamson, M. A., and Wholey, J. S. "Organization and Management of the Evaluation Function in a Multilevel Organization." In R. J. Wooldridge (ed.), *Evaluation of Complex Systems.* New Directions for Program Evaluation, no. 10. San Francisco: Jossey-Bass, 1981.

Alchian, A. A., and Demsetz, H. "Production, Information Costs, and Economic Organization." *American Economic Review,* 1972, *62* (5), 777–795.

Alkin, M. C., and Ruskus, J. *Reflections on Evaluation Costs: Direct and Indirect.* Los Angeles: Center for the Study of Evaluation, University of California, 1984.

Alkin, M. C., and Solmon, L. C. (eds.). *The Costs of Evaluation.* Newbury Park, Calif.: Sage, 1983.

Alkin, M. C., and Stecher, B. "A Study of Evaluation Costs." In M. C. Alkin and L. C. Solmon (eds.), *The Costs of Evaluation.* Newbury Park, Calif.: Sage, 1983.

Armstrong, R. L. "The Intangible Costs and Benefits of School Self-Study." *The North Central Association Quarterly,* 1982, *57,* 395–401.

Bowen, H. R. *Evaluating Institutions for Accountability.* San Francisco: Jossey-Bass, 1974.

Bowen, H. R. *The Costs of Higher Education: How Much Do Colleges and Universities Spend Per Student and How Much Should They Spend?* San Francisco: Jossey-Bass, 1980.

Bowen, H. R. "The Reform of Undergraduate Education: Estimated Costs." Paper presented at Wingspread Conference, Racine, Wisconsin, 1985.

Catterall, J. S. "A Theoretical Model for Examining the Costs of Testing." In M. C. Alkin and L. C. Solmon (eds.), *The Costs of Evaluation.* Newbury Park, Calif.: Sage, 1983.

Chambers, J. G., and Parrish, T. B. *The Development of a Program Cost Model and a Cost of Education Model for the State of Alaska.* Palo Alto, Calif.: Associates for Education Finance and Planning, Stanford Press, 1984.

Cleveland, H. *The Costs and Benefits of Openness: Sunshine Laws and Higher Education.* Washington, D.C.: Association of Governing Boards of Universities and Colleges, 1985.

Conrad, E. F., and Wilson, R. F. *Academic Program Reviews: Institutional Approaches, Expectations, and Controversies.* ASHE-ERIC Higher Education Report no. 5. Washington, D.C.: Association for the Study of Higher Education, 1985.

Day, G. S. "Assessing the Effects of Information Disclosure Requirements." In D. A. Aaker and G. S. Day (eds.), *Consumerism: Search for the Consumer Interest.* New York: The Free Press, 1978.

Decision Analysis Group. *Readings in Decision Analysis.* Menlo Park, Calif.: Stanford Research Institute, 1976.

Dornbusch, S. M. "Perspectives from Sociology: Organizational Evaluation of Faculty Performances." In D. R. Lewis and W. E. Becker, Jr. (eds.), *Academic Rewards in Higher Education.* Cambridge, Mass.: Ballinger, 1979.

Drezek, S., Monkowski, P. G., and Higgins, P. S. "Current vs. Perceived-Ideal Procedures for Determining Educational Program-Evaluation Budgets: A Survey of School Evaluators." *Educational Evaluation and Policy Analysis,* 1982, *4* (1), 97–108.

Ewell, P. T., and Jones, D. P. "The Costs of Assessment." Paper prepared for the National Center for Higher Education Management Systems, Boulder, Colorado, 1985.

Haggart, S. A. "Determining the Resource Requirements and Cost of Evaluation." In M. C. Alkin and L. C. Solmon (eds.), *The Costs of Evaluation.* Newbury Park, Calif.: Sage, 1983.

Halstead, D. K. *Higher Education Prices and Price Indexes.* DHEW Publication no. OE 75-17005. Washington, D.C.: U.S. Government Printing Office, 1975.

Hirschleifer, J. "The Private and Social Value of Information and the Reward to Inventive Activity." *American Economic Review,* 1971, *61* (4), 561–574.

Huber, G. P. *Managerial Decision Making.* Glenview, Ill.: Scott, Foresman and Company, 1980.

Joint Committee on Standards for Educational Evaluation. *Standards for Evaluations of Educational Programs, Projects, and Materials.* New York: McGraw-Hill, 1981.

Levin, H. M. *Cost-Effectiveness: A Primer.* Newbury Park, Calif.: Sage, 1983.

Lewis, D. R., and Wasescha, A. M. "Costs and Benefits of Assessment in Post-Secondary Education." Paper presented at annual meeting of the Association for the Study of Higher Education, San Diego, Feb. 16, 1987.

Morell, J. A., and Weirich, T. W. "Determining the Costs of Evaluation: Principles from Mental Health." In M. C. Alkin and L. C. Solmon (eds.), *The Costs of Evaluation.* Newbury Park, Calif.: Sage, 1983.

National Association of College and University Business Officers. *Fundamental Considerations for Determining Cost Information in Higher Education.* Washington, D.C.: National Association of College and University Business Officers, 1977.

Popham, W. J. *Educational Evaluation.* Englewood Cliffs, N.J.: Prentice-Hall, 1975.

Rusnell, D. "Cost-Effective Evaluation: Is There a $500 Solution for a $1,000 Problem?" In A. B. Knox (ed.), *Assessing the Impact of Continuing Education.* New Directions for Continuing Education, no. 3. San Francisco: Jossey-Bass, 1979.

Scriven, M. "Costs in Evaluation: Concept and Practice." In M. C. Alkin and L. C. Solmon (eds.), *The Costs of Evaluation.* Newbury Park, Calif.: Sage, 1983.

Seeley, J. "Program Review and Evaluation." In N. L. Poulton (ed.), *Evaluation of Management and Planning Systems.* San Francisco: Jossey-Bass, 1981.

Stigler, G. S. "The Economics of Information." *Journal of Political Economy,* 1961, *69* (3), 213–225.

Trow, M. "The Public and Private Lives of Higher Education." *Daedelus,* 1975, *104* (1), 113–127.

Verry, D., and Davies, B. *University Costs and Outputs.* Amsterdam: Elsevier, 1976.

Webster, W. J., and Stufflebeam, D. L. "The State of Theory and Practice in Educational Evaluation in Large Urban School Districts." Paper presented at annual meeting of the American Educational Research Association, Toronto, March 1978.

Darrell R. Lewis is professor of educational policy and administration at the University of Minnesota.

Tennessee's performance-funding policy rewards public institutions for undertaking comprehensive assessment programs. New policy guidelines emphasize such quantitative indicators as test scores and alumni ratings.

Assessment as an Instrument of State Funding Policy

Trudy W. Banta

In the relatively recent history of state initiatives for the assessment and improvement of quality in higher education, Tennessee is a pioneer. In 1975–1976, the Tennessee Higher Education Commission (THEC) initiated discussions concerning the feasibility of allocating a portion of state funds for higher education on the basis of performance criteria, rather than using an enrollment-based formula. During 1976–1977, pilot projects were carried out on twelve campuses to test the viability of collecting and using data related to a variety of performance indicators. In 1979, a supplement amounting of 2 percent of the instructional component of the education and general (E and G) budget for each institution was added to the statewide appropriation for higher education to reward institutions that undertook assessment programs and compiled the results in annual reports submitted with the institutional budget requests.

Initial Guidelines for Performance Funding

In 1979, the performance criteria to be addressed in institutions' annual reports were outlined in a brief set of guidelines. The THEC staff, in consultation with a group of institutional representatives, later tightened the guidelines (1983) and committed the state to a five-year

T. W. Banta (ed.). *Implementing Outcomes Assessment: Promise and Perils.*
New Directions for Institutional Research, no. 59. San Francisco: Jossey-Bass, Fall 1988.

performance-funding program. Beginning in 1983, the awarding of points and the appropriation of funds were based on the following criteria:

1. *Accreditation.* This criterion concerned the percentage of programs eligible for accreditation that were accredited.

2. *Program Field Evaluation.* This criterion focused on the percentage of programs that had undergone peer review and/or administered comprehensive field exams to majors within a five-year period. Maximum credit for this standard was awarded if an exam was used and if student performance either improved over time or exceeded the performance of students in similar programs at comparable institutions.

3. *Institutionwide Educational Outcomes.* This criterion dealt with measurement of value added, via the general education component of the curriculum, on the basis of the ACT COMP exam. Maximum credit was awarded if the performance of seniors either improved over time or exceeded that of seniors at a group of comparable institutions.

4. *Referent Group Surveys.* This criterion reflected the use of surveys of enrolled students, alumni, community members, and/or employers to determine quality of academic programs and services. Institutions were expected to demonstrate that findings had been used to suggest specific improvements.

5. *Planning for Instructional Improvement.* This criterion concerned implementation of a campuswide plan for instructional improvement based on information derived from the procedures described here, as well as from other sources.

The THEC staff assigned a total of 100 points to these standards: 25 for full accomplishment of the first, 30 for the second, 25 for the third, and 10 each for the fourth and fifth. Along with the increase in specifications for obtaining the performance-funding supplement came an increase in the amount of the supplement. In 1983, the annual appropriation for performance funding grew from 2 to 5 percent of the E and G budget for each institution.

Tennessee was the first state to provide a financial incentive for public institutions to undertake assessment activities, but Virginia and New Jersey followed in 1984, as others did later. No state has enacted a prescription for meeting the requirements for incentive funding as detailed as Tennessee's. Early critics even charged that the policy was so intrusive that faculty would chafe under the requirements, and that Tennessee's *enfant terrible* would not survive.

Nevertheless, the first formal five-year cycle of Tennessee's performance-funding program has been completed, and in 1986 the THEC voted to continue it for another five years. In institutions as diverse as the ones that are subject to the policy—Tennessee's technical institutes, two-year community colleges, regional universities, and research institution—what have been the positive and negative features of implementing each of the performance-funding criteria? What factors have allowed this policy to endure?

Strengths and Weaknesses of Initial Performance-Funding Guidelines

Near the end of the first five-year funding cycle, the present author sent a nine-page questionnaire on performance funding to the president of each of Tennessee's twenty-three publicly supported institutions. Responses came in from every campus. The following paragraphs describe the strengths and weaknesses that respondents associated with each of the five performance-funding criteria.

Accreditation. At more than half of Tennessee's postsecondary institutions, a larger percentage of programs was accredited in 1987 than was the case before performance funding was initiated. A third of these campuses acknowledged the influence of performance funding. Most of the institutions thus motivated considered the decision to seek accreditation as one with long-range positive consequences. Two related objections to accreditation were cited, however: The criteria of an accrediting body may not be congruent with the mission of the institution or with the objectives of the department to which they apply; and the pursuit of accreditation may cause resources to be directed toward a given unit, when in fact the mission of the institution would be furthered by using the funds in some other way.

Program Field Evaluation. Performance funding caused the number of institutions using formal peer-review processes to quadruple. The number of institutions testing students with comprehensive exams in their major fields also increased dramatically. By the end of the five-year cycle, all twenty-three institutions had tested majors in 80 to 100 percent of their program fields. At one institution, only locally developed exams were used; all other institutions employed combinations of standardized and locally developed exams. Of the seventeen institutions that valued one kind more than the other, 59 percent favored the locally developed tests and 41 percent preferred standardized exams. Faculty developing their own exams gained from their involvement in the process and learned more about program weaknesses, but faculty using standardized exams often felt more confident about their results, because their exams were externally validated and provided norms for comparative purposes.

Institutionwide Educational Outcomes. All four-year institutions and community colleges had begun to give the ACT COMP exam to graduates to assess achievement in general education, and 70 percent of these schools believed the testing was worth the time and expense because they valued the information it provided about the curriculum.

Referent Group Surveys. This performance-funding criterion stimulated interest in the systematic collection of data via surveys. More referent groups were surveyed more often, with more detailed instruments than had ever previously been the case at any institution. Moreover, since the criterion specified that survey information should be used to focus program-improvement efforts, faculty and administrators alike took the surveys seriously and were guided by the findings. Twenty of the institutions felt that the benefits of using the surveys outweighed the costs in institutional time and effort.

Planning for Instructional Improvement. The number of Tennessee institutions using comprehensive institutional planning processes more than doubled during the first cycle of performance funding. All institutions favored retaining some form of this criterion in the new five-year plan. Several considered it the most important of all criteria, since it ensured that the collection of assessment data would not be an end in itself, but rather that campus decision makers would use the information derived, in combination with that from other sources, to improve programs and services.

Responses of the Tennessee institutional presidents reveal that a number of significant achievements were stimulated by this policy, whose critics initially viewed it as a threat to institutional autonomy and academic freedom. The overall impact of performance funding was considered positive by 95 percent of Tennessee's postsecondary institutions. Even the one institution that reported an overall negative impact described positive actions taken in response to at least one of the funding criteria.

The most favorable reactions concerned the availability (from surveys) of improved institution-specific information, faculty involvement in test development, and the impetus to use assessment data in planning for improvement. Institutions were not inclined to use accreditation as an indicator of program quality, but the most negative reactions concerned the weight given to exams in general education and in major fields that faculty did not consider valid for assessing curricula. Standardized exams may be useful in providing extrainstitutional data for comparative purposes, but they are unlikely to be congruent with all of a given faculty's objectives for student development. This fact, coupled with the absence of detailed information about student performance, makes it very difficult to base program improvements on the results of most standardized tests.

These findings indicate that performance funding is a viable policy for assessing the ability of programs to meet their objectives for student development and for stimulating activities designed to improve programs and services.

Success Factors

Factors that contributed to the survival of Tennessee's policy during its early phases include the following:

1. Participation in performance funding was voluntary; thus, it was not viewed as coercive by either faculty or administrators.
2. Performance funding was a budgetary supplement granted for providing evidence of program quality and efforts to improve programs; institutional funds were not taken away for noncompliance or for poor performance.
3. The supplement was large enough to encourage institutions to overcome internal and external barriers to assessment.
4. Institutional representatives participated in formulating the guidelines.
5. Performance funding was phased in so that faculty and administrators had time to make adjustments gradually, often incorporating assessment activities into ongoing programs.
6. The criteria were somewhat flexible and encouraged institutional innovation. Institutions were permitted to construct their own survey instruments and exams in major fields and to devise their own plans for improvement, based on evaluative findings.
7. Institutions did not compete with one another for funds; each institution was entitled to the full 5 percent supplement, set aside for its exclusive use, if it met the performance criteria.
8. Perhaps most important, undue emphasis was not placed on the levels of test scores, which may reflect innate ability more than growth or development promoted by the college experience. Instead, the performance-funding criteria rewarded evidence of student score gain, as promoted by the curriculum, and the use of data to suggest improvements.

Revision of Performance Funding Guidelines (1987)

While the performance-funding policy that took effect early in the decade was gaining acceptance as a stimulus for program improvement on campuses across the state, it was also winning approval from legislators and the members of the THEC as an instrument for holding institutions accountable for the expenditure of public funds. As colleges developed an appreciation for the survey and planning processes encouraged by the policy, lawmakers and the gubernatorial appointees to the THEC were increasingly impressed with the potential offered by tests and consumer ratings for comparing and ranking institutions in terms of their effectiveness as stewards of state funds.

In 1986, when the THEC membership was given the opportunity to discontinue or renew performance funding, the decision to extend the policy for five more years was made readily, with widespread support from commissioners appointed by Democratic and Republican governors alike. Seven academic leaders representing the state's public institutions were asked to join the governing board and the THEC staff in improving the guidelines for the five-year cycle scheduled to begin July 1, 1987.

Throughout a full year of discussions, committee members dealt continually with at least two sets of tensions. The first set concerned the value that institutions placed on survey and planning processes, versus the importance that quantitative reporting had for the THEC. The second set included conflicts that inevitably develop among institutions that pursue different missions under diverse styles of leadership. As anticipated, what ultimately resulted was a set of guidelines that contained many compromises. Everyone involved could point to some small victory, but no one was completely satisfied with the document.

The 1987 performance-funding guidelines included essentially the same components as the earlier version had, but new titles for standards—formerly called criteria—and a different weighting structure were employed, as follows: (1) Accreditation—20 points, down from 25; (2) Major Field Assessment—maintained at 30 points; (3) Undergraduate General Education Outcomes—20 points, rather than 25; (4) Satisfaction Surveys—increased from 10 to 15 points; and (5) Corrective Measures (Planning for Instructional Improvement)—increased from 10 to 15 points. In addition, the 1987 guidelines incorporated a sixth criterion, permitting institutions to earn up to 10 points of extra credit over five years by pilot testing new assessment instruments. The paragraphs that follow discuss the strengths and weaknesses of the new guidelines from a campus perspective.

Accreditation. The weighting of Standard I was reduced, because accreditation by professional associations may indicate only that certain minimal standards have been met, and not that noteworthy outcomes have been achieved. Moreover, institutions that have accreditable programs for which they do not wish to pursue accreditation may now request exemptions for a small number of such programs.

Institutional representatives viewed most of the changes in the accreditation standard positively. Nevertheless, a few maintained that a criterion based on program accreditation has no place in a set of qualitative criteria that are used to determine institutional funding levels. These critics may be mollified somewhat in future years as the U.S. Department of Education's (1987) new guidelines for approval of accrediting agencies begin to require that outcomes assessment be one of each agency's accreditation criteria.

Major Field Assessment. The purpose of the new performance-

Table 1. Scoring for Licensing/Certification Exams

Increase in Percent of Students Scoring Above National Mean	less than 2.0	2.0 to 2.9	3.0 to 3.9	4.0 to 4.9	5.0 or more
Percent			*Points*		
51 or more	10	10	10	10	10
47 to 50	6	8	10	10	10
40 to 46	4	6	8	10	10
30 to 39	2	4	6	8	10
fewer than 30	0	2	4	6	8

Source: Tennessee Higher Education Commission, 1987.

funding Standard II for Tennessee's universities is to reward quality of major field programs, as indicated by "(1) the performance of graduating students on approved undergraduate major field tests; and (2) external review of master's programs" (Tennessee Higher Education Commission, 1987, p. 5). For scoring purposes, some major fields in which licensing or certification exams are available will be assessed twice during the five-year cycle, on the basis of scores obtained by graduating students on the appropriate tests. Scores will be evaluated both by level of student performance, relative to the national mean on the exam, and by extent of improvement over the previous performance of record (see Table 1.)

Other major fields, not subject to licensing or certification examination requirements, will be assessed once (for reporting purposes) during the five-year cycle via performance of graduating students on approved tests. These tests may be nationally normed, locally developed by faculty at a single institution, or developed cooperatively by several institutions.

According to the guidelines, the following scoring procedures will apply: "A major field program will be considered successful if the mean score of all examinees (1) exceeds a recognized norm or (2) has improved over the last previous performance of record. An institution's score . . . will be determined by its cumulative success rate, i.e., the total number of successes during a cycle divided by the number of major fields tested to date, including retests, during the same cycle" (Tennessee Higher Education Commission, 1987, p. 7; see Table 2).

Each of an institution's master's-degree programs will be assessed once during the five-year performance-funding cycle, on the basis of a review conducted by at least one external consultant in the discipline. Over a period of years, the Tennessee Conference of Graduate Schools (TCGS), a group composed of graduate deans at Tennessee universities, has developed a set of qualitative standards for master's-degree programs (Minkel and Richards, 1986). To accommodate the quantitative thrust of

Table 2. Scoring for Other Major Fields

Percent of Successful Programs	0 to 35.9	36.0 to 45.9	46.0 to 54.9	55.0 to 62.9	63.0 to 69.9	70.0 to 74.9	75.0 to 79.9	80.0 to 100
Points	0	2	4	6	7	8	9	10

Source: Tennessee Higher Education Commission, 1987.

Table 3. Scoring for Master's Degree Programs—Objective Standards

Number of Standards Met	1-2	3-5	6-7	8	9	10
Points	0	3	4	5	6	7

Source: Tennessee Higher Education Commission, 1987.

Standard II, a checklist was devised for use by the external reviewer. It lists these qualitative standards, with numerical values assigned to each.

The first section of the checklist sets out ten criteria of graduate programs that the reviewer must judge as "met" or "not met." The list includes such items as screening and supervision of students, availability and sophistication of coursework, comprehensive examination, and culminating experience. According to the guidelines, "Each major field program will be given a score from 0 to 7 depending on the number of TCGS standards met. . . . To calculate the institutional score for the purpose of this Standard, the scores of all major fields assessed in a given year will be averaged and rounded to the nearest whole number" (Tennessee Higher Education Commission, 1987, p. 8; see Table 3).

Finally, the external reviewer is asked to use a four-position scale (3-excellent, 2-good, 1-minimally acceptable, 0-poor) to evaluate the master's program on overall quality of students' learning experience, faculty quality, quality of the teaching and learning environment, and quality and use of program evaluation. The average of these ratings for a program calculated "to one decimal will constitute the program's score. Individual program scores will be again averaged . . . to establish the institution's total score for this standard" (Tennessee Higher Education Commission, 1987, p. 8).

Clearly, the strong desire of the THEC members and staff that the performance-funding guidelines permit counting and scoring, and—by extension—comparing and ranking of institutions, was accommodated in the construction of Standard II, but institutions also achieved two goals in the deliberations. First, credit is given not only for high scores but also for score improvements, so that an institution whose students do not achieve the national average on a standardized exam can still be rewarded if scores have improved over time. Second, a way was found to give institutions credit for conducting program reviews (which, in the eyes of many academics, are the quintessential assessment technique). Initially, discussions about including program review as a component of the standards had been complicated by the difficulty of evaluating the reviews objectively for scoring purposes.

Despite the compromises that have accommodated institutional perspectives, colleges and universities still find serious deficiencies in Standard II. First, exams developed by professional associations to regulate entry into the professions are not intended for use in evaluating programs. Items on these tests are selected for their power to discriminate among the highest and lowest scorers, not to ascertain what proportion of a given class of students has mastered the skills considered important by the faculty of a particular institution. The potential for misusing tests designed to discriminate among individuals in assessing the performance of groups has led some professional organizations to take action, and others to consider doing so, to place new limits on the information supplied to institutions about their students' performance on licensing or certification exams. Tennessee institutions will be at a particular disadvantage as they try to evaluate scores on licensing exams in several professional fields. They must require *all* graduating students—regardless of ability, motivation, or future career plans—to take the exams but then must compare students' average scores with national norms, based on scores achieved by students at other institutions who volunteered to take exams and were motivated by their desire to gain entry into a profession.

Second, while it is desirable to include improvement in test scores as a criterion of program quality, improvement is very difficult to measure accurately. The largest component of student performance on any test is innate ability, and this factor must be considered as test scores of a senior class in one year are compared with scores achieved on the same test by a later senior class. No provision for statistically treating differences due to varying levels of student ability is included in the new guidelines, and because the size of many of the classes being tested is small (fewer than twenty students), use of such procedures with these groups would be inappropriate, in any case.

Having program review recognized by being included in the standards is a positive development, and the use of program review as an assessment technique is far more appropriate for master's-degree programs than was the previous practice of reporting a single mean test score as an indicator of program quality. Nevertheless, Tennessee's graduate deans participated somewhat reluctantly in adapting their carefully crafted set of qualitative standards for use as a checklist for assigning scores to programs. In this case, the whole is much more than the sum of its parts. As they arrive at their own assessments of program quality and determine the actions needed to improve it, institutions will derive more guidance from the narrative reports provided by reviewers than from the sum of points from the THEC checklist.

Undergraduate General Education Outcomes. Standard III is designed to reward an institution for the quality of its undergraduate general education program, as indicated by the performance of graduating students on the ACT COMP exam. Despite the fact that institutions have found few significant relationships between the general education experiences they provide and students' performance on this exam, the exam does offer subscores that appear to measure important aspects of general education, and ACT offers a convenient method for estimating a mean value-added score that permits interinstitutional comparisons. Thus, the ACT COMP was retained as the approved instrument for Standard III by those seeking additional quantification in the new performance funding schedule. Institutions did receive accommodations in Standard III. Those with a history of administering the COMP exam to freshmen were permitted to use longitudinal gain scores rather than the ACT estimates in reporting value added. In addition, part of the score for Standard III is based on actual score (national percentile rank), rather than on the value-added score alone, as was the case until 1987. Another point of contention with institutions was eliminated when the all-or-nothing basis for meeting the value-added standard was changed to a sliding scale that awards partial credit even for minimal mean-score gain. Finally, the value of Standard III was reduced from 25 to 20 points, a concession that showed further recognition of institutions' dissatisfaction with the use of the ACT COMP exam.

Satisfaction Surveys. The purpose of Standard IV is to reward institutions for administering a common survey instrument semiannually to alumni two years out and for exceeding state norms (or national norms based on institutional size for some items) for level of satisfaction or showing improvement over the last previous performance of record. In years when the alumni survey is not given, a survey of dropouts will be conducted.

A committee composed of three institutional representatives and of THEC and governing board staff developed an alumni survey and adapted it, by changing only the institution name throughout, for use by each state college and university. A common methodology for administering the questionnaire by mail and electronically recording the responses was prescribed. Data analysis will be handled centrally by state data-processing specialists.

With the exception of demographic questions, responses to all survey items will be counted in the scoring process. Using response means, state averages for each item will be calculated for two- and four-year institutions. National norms will be used for comparison on those

Table 4. Scoring for Surveys

Percent of Items Successful (Above State or National Average)	40–54	55–69	70–79	80 or more
Points	6	10	13	15

Source: Tennessee Higher Education Commission, 1987.

items for which they are available. Table 4 shows how an institution's score will be determined.

Institutions have been able to use survey data more readily than scores from most tests to suggest directions for improving programs. For this reason, there was high institutional interest in maintaining a standard that concerned surveys and increasing its weight in the performance-funding guidelines. THEC members and staff were disinclined to continue awarding credit for surveys, however, because it was difficult to score the results objectively. In the compromise that was effected, surveys were retained and given greater weight, and a way to quantify the results was developed.

Institutional representatives have greeted gains on Standard IV with mixed emotions. A useful tool—the alumni survey—will receive performance-funding credit, but no way has yet been found (although the door has been left ajar for further work in this area) to reward institutions that undertake any other kinds of surveys, several of which would be more productive than alumni surveys for suggesting institutional improvements. Standard IV encourages institutions to conduct surveys of dropouts in alternate years, but they will get no credit for doing so. No mention is made of surveying enrolled students, employers, and others.

The proposed method of using state norms for survey responses troubles institutions. By definition, half the colleges in each category will score below the two- or four-year state average, and politicians and the press undoubtedly will take full advantage of the rare opportunity the method affords for making direct comparisons of institutions that have quite diverse missions.

Corrective Measures. Its new title, developed by THEC members, belies the positive implications that Standard V has for institutions. Standard V is designed to reward institutions for undertaking three kinds of programmatic improvements: immediate changes, the need for which is identified through the testing and surveying initiatives specified in Standards II, III, IV; strategic instructional initiatives intended to address broader institutional goals over one, two, or three years; and substantial institutional innovations requiring longer-term commitments. Scoring for the first type of improvement will be based on the percentage of identified needs that prompt the institution to take responsive action; for the second and third types, scoring will be based on the extent to which needed improvements are planned, implemented, and evaluated.

As with Standard IV, institutions were in favor of retaining planning for instructional improvement and giving it more weight in the guidelines, while THEC staff and members were reluctant to include it because of the difficulty of scoring narrative descriptions of improvements. The institutions were granted the right to receive increased credit for planning, but in the bargain they accepted another quantification strategy. Institutions scoring below a specified level on Standard III will now be judged on Standard V according to their actions to improve scores on the subscales of the ACT COMP exam; but since COMP scores have not been linked definitively to specific aspects of curriculum or instruction, the kinds of actions needed to improve these scores are unknown. Moreover, programs reporting performance below the national average on a standardized exam in a major field must now demonstrate that appropriate improvement actions have been taken. Unfortunately, the only information institutions receive about student performance on many of these tests is the percentage that passed, or a single overall score. Such data provide no clues concerning appropriate improvement actions.

Developing and Piloting Assessment Instruments. Standard VI provides extra credit to institutions for developing and/or pilot-testing new assessment instruments. Obviously, this opportunity to experiment with alternative measurement approaches is appealing. In early attempts to use this option, however, THEC staff have not approved any procedure that would involve temporarily suspending a provision of Standards I through V. Thus, it is not clear that Standard VI will produce opportunities for true experiments.

Promise and Perils of Using Assessment in Funding

The higher education community has watched with interest Tennessee's bold experiment in linking funding with qualitative indicators. Some educators winced in 1979 at the news that a state was beginning to award public funds on the basis of performance above the national average on standardized tests and estimates of value added derived from COMP exam scores, but it was clear to those who studied the guidelines for performance funding that institutions could receive substantial rewards simply for undertaking assessment activities. The emphasis placed on levels of test scores was not excessive. The early phases of the initiative, guided by a general outline that was coupled with a substantial financial incentive for institutions to engage in certain broad processes of assessment, yielded positive results for institutions and pleased state officials. Although the 1987 guidelines have been official policy for only a short time, it seems reasonable to assume that, broadly construed, they will lead to further campus improvements and ultimately to higher institutional quality in Tennessee.

During the process of producing the new performance-funding guidelines, however, palpable tension developed between, on the one hand, institutions' desire to look at THEC-specified assessment data in a broad, general way as one (but not the only) source of information about program quality and how to improve it, and, on the other, the desire of state policymakers to focus on test scores and survey responses as if they constituted what Peter Ewell has called "perfect data." For virtually every valued process that educators won the right to retain in the 1987 guidelines, they accepted a quantitative evaluation method for scoring purposes. The result will make it much easier, although not more appropriate, to compare institutions with missions as different as that of a community college and that of a research university. As a single test score average comes to mean thousands of dollars to an institution, pressure to improve that score inevitably will be brought to bear on faculty, and curricula may be narrowed to accommodate special emphasis on the material contained in the test.

Tennessee is unique in its prescriptive approach to encouraging assessment at public institutions. Tennessee is not unique in possessing elected and appointed decision makers at the state level who can be persuaded that test scores, survey responses, and a wide variety of scaled variables can be used to rate and rank institutions.

Certainly, the state has both the right and the obligation to stipulate the standards on which funding for public institutions will be allocated. Assessment data can yield some objective evidence of the effectiveness of colleges and universities in meeting those standards. Much to the state's credit, Tennessee has provided essential money and encouragement for higher education to enter wholeheartedly into institution-wide assessment programs, the results of which can yield increased efficiency and responsiveness to students' needs. As more institutions across the country take steps to implement assessment programs that offer the promise of directing institutional improvement, they must be aware of the perils associated with collecting data that can be used for comparative purposes, and they must simultaneously try to acquaint decision makers with the limitations of such data.

References

Minkel, C. W., and Richards, M. P. *Components of Quality in Master's Degree Programs.* Knoxville: Tennessee Conference of Graduate Schools, 1986.
Tennessee Higher Education Commission. *Instructional Evaluation Variables, November, 1983.* Nashville: Tennessee Higher Education Commission, 1983.
Tennessee Higher Education Commission. *Performance Funding Standards for Public Colleges and Universities, July 1, 1987.* Nashville: Tennessee Higher Education Commission, 1987.

U.S. Department of Education. "Secretary's Procedures and Criteria for Recognition of Accrediting Agencies." *Federal Register*, 1987, *52* (173), 33906–33913.

Trudy W. Banta is research professor in the Learning Research Center and director of the Assessment Resource Center at the University of Tennessee, Knoxville.

*Institutional researchers must bring measurement theorists
and assessment practitioners together to develop new and
more suitable methods for assessing developmental
changes in groups of students.*

Promise and Perils

Trudy W. Banta

We began this sourcebook with the assumption that conscientious implementation of comprehensive campus assessment programs holds promise
for institutions. This point has been amply illustrated by the experiences
of Alverno College, Northeast Missouri State University, James Madison
University, Kean College, King's College, and the University of Tennessee,
Knoxville, to name a few of the institutions that have taken assessment
seriously. At these and other institutions around the country, numerous
assessment initiatives are producing positive consequences for students
and faculty.

Positive Consequences of Assessment

The ultimate objective of an assessment program is to track the
intellectual and social development of individual students, from college
entry to graduation and even beyond. Student progress through the curriculum can be monitored and findings shared so that individuals can
take positive actions to improve their rates of growth. Collectively, the
performance of students on comprehensive exams can inform faculty
about the strengths and weaknesses of curricula designed to promote
student development toward goals faculty consider important. Students'
evaluations of curricula, of instructional methods, and of student services
can also be used to suggest directions for improvement.

T. W. Banta (ed.). *Implementing Outcomes Assessment: Promise and Perils.*
New Directions for Institutional Research, no. 59. San Francisco: Jossey-Bass, Fall 1988.

Assessment data are being used in combination with information from other sources to help external consultants draw inferences about program quality in comprehensive program reviews. Campus administrators and faculty value the objective data gained from assessment procedures and program reviews in providing direction for decisions about investing institutional resources to correct weaknesses and to promote excellence. Taken together, evaluations of all its individual programs yield some evidence of an institution's effectiveness. Public officials, lawmakers, taxpayers, parents, and students welcome results of assessment that demonstrate an institution's accountability for the use of public funds and its concern about ensuring the quality of its services.

Despite the many potential benefits of assessment, however, there are also drawbacks. The authors featured in this volume have attempted to describe some of the most important ones.

Negative Aspects of Assessment

Largely because of pressure from external sources, assessment activities have often been started without thorough review of all the related research. Moreover, since assessment is a complex, multidisciplinary undertaking, there is an enormous amount of research to study and synthesize. In an obviously related field, educational measurement, for example, state-of-the-art commercially available instruments do not provide the kind of measurement that is really needed. As Warren (Chapter Three) and Hanson (Chapter Five) have pointed out, we have used tests designed to measure *individual differences* with respect to *static traits* to draw conclusions about how *groups* of students *change* as a result of their college experiences. In fact, the more reliable or stable a test is for assessing individual differences on a given trait (that is, the more likely a student is to achieve the same score if taking the test on two different occasions), the less reliable are the change scores it produces.

In some cases, policymakers have ignored the considerable research on the process of change and have suggested that groups of diverse institutions simply adopt the assessment model that had been successful at a given college or university. In search of perfect data or the so-called single indicator of quality (see Ewell's chapter in this volume), we have relied on single scores or ratings; we have adopted simple research designs to study direct effects, when we actually needed complex designs to tell us about indirect as well as direct effects of educational experiences. Lewis (Chapter Six) has alerted us to the potential danger of providing evaluation results to external agencies in simplified and trivialized forms: Recipients of such information may use it to increase their role in making decisions that would more properly be made within individual institutions.

Minimizing the Negative and Accentuating the Positive

The need for assessing and improving higher education cannot be ignored, nor can action be postponed, until perfectly acceptable instruments and methods are developed. Miller (Chapter One) believes we have from three to five years to take advantage of policymakers' interest and obtain the resources we need for creditable assessment programs and the attendant improvement efforts. He suggests that we employ what we know about promoting change in diverse, complex institutions to adapt existing assessment models for new use on individual campuses.

Ewell emphasizes that each institution must determine its own purpose for assessment. This purpose guides the selection of instruments and the timing of data collection and ensures that the results of an assessment are used. Details of implementation necessarily vary according to the mission, the organizational framework, and the prevailing leadership style of the institution, as well as the competence of the faculty, and the abilities and interests of the students.

Warren recommends that we build upon the accepted practice of testing students in their courses to accomplish the purposes of assessment. If faculty in one discipline develop their own comprehensive exams, perhaps in cooperation with faculty in the same discipline at peer institutions, the exams can be divided into parts, with each part administered to a sample of students as part of course exams. Testing time will be minimized, student motivation to do well will be enhanced, and faculty will have a vested interest in using the results of the assessment.

Hanson's chapter furnishes an illustration of Ewell's single-indicator fallacy. Hanson poses a question: Which students change, and in what ways, when they are exposed to what kinds of educational experiences? To answer, we need more information than can be communicated by a single mean test score. Data for subgroups must be analyzed, because an educational technique that is effective with eighteen-year-old males, for example, may not work at all with forty-five-year-old females. To indicate more about when and how change occurs, assessment should take place at several points during the student's career. As Lewis reminds us, however, before undertaking an elaborate multistage assessment design, we should carefully weigh its costs, and those of alternative procedures, against the potential value of the information to be derived from each approach.

Institutional researchers and administrators have a strategic role to play in helping assessment realize its promise. First, we can impress upon the campus assessment committee how important it is to review related literature and to use data-collection designs that permit analysis of the differential effects of college experiences on particular subgroups of students and on students with a variety of learning styles and personality types. Second, we can bring measurement theorists and assessment practitioners together to develop new and more suitable methods for assessing developmental changes in groups of students. Third, as better instruments and procedures become available, we can improve our practice by incorporating them as quickly as prudence allows into campus assessment programs. Finally, we can help campus leaders convince state policymakers that financial resources should be made available to carry out broad-based assessment programs. These will not simply yield a few mean test scores and ratings; rather, they will provide a variety of information to guide campus improvements and make institutions more effective and responsive to the needs of society.

Trudy W. Banta is research professor in the Learning Research Center and director of the Assessment Resource Center at the University of Tennessee, Knoxville.

Before beginning assessment programs, institutions should carefully examine the literature on assessment practice, including the experiences of other institutions.

An Annotated Bibliography and Program Descriptions

Gary R. Pike

Over the last five years, interest in assessing student educational outcomes has increased dramatically in this country. This growing interest has been fueled in large part by state laws and accreditation requirements. There has also been a parallel growth in the literature on assessment. In view of the variety of information currently available, this bibliography is not exhaustive. Instead, it provides a starting point for the study of assessment.

Sources on Assessment

Adelman, C. P. (ed.). *Assessment in American Higher Education: Issues and Contexts.* Washington, D.C.: U.S. Government Printing Office, 1985.
> This series of essays, based on presentations made at the First National Conference on Assessment in Higher Education, examines assessment from a variety of perspectives, including the philosophy of assessment, assessment in professional/technical schools, selection of assessment instruments, and evaluating the costs of assessment.

Astin, A. W. *Achieving Educational Excellence: A Critical Assessment of Priorities and Practices in Higher Education.* San Francisco: Jossey-Bass, 1985.

T. W. Banta (ed.). *Implementing Outcomes Assessment: Promise and Perils.*
New Directions for Institutional Research, no. 59. San Francisco: Jossey-Bass, Fall 1988.

Astin examines the concept of quality in higher education. He begins by identifying some limitations of the traditional indicators of quality, and he advocates the use of a talent-development (value-added) approach to assessing quality. Using data from the Cooperative Institutional Research Program (CIRP), Astin suggests several steps institutions can take to promote educational quality.

Banta, T. W. (ed.). *Performance Funding in Higher Education: A Critical Analysis of Tennessee's Experience.* Boulder, Colo.: National Center for Higher Education Management Systems, 1986.

Tennessee's performance-funding initiative serves as the focal point of the essays in this volume. The topics include policy issues (such as the development of performance-funding criteria and the use of data in institutional planning) and measurement issues (such as using surveys to measure student satisfaction, and testing achievement in general education and in the major).

Bergquist, W. H., and Armstrong, J. R. *Planning Effectively for Educational Quality: An Outcomes-Based Approach for Colleges Committed to Excellence.* San Francisco: Jossey-Bass, 1986.

In providing a model for improving educational quality, the authors urge institutions to examine their missions, develop pilot programs designed to assist in accomplishing those missions, assess the effectiveness of the pilot programs, and then implement large-scale programs. They stress the importance of incorporating outcomes data into the planning process.

Berk, R. A. (ed.). *Performance Assessment: Methods and Applications.* Baltimore, Md.: Johns Hopkins University Press, 1986.

This volume is a basic reference work on performance assessment. Authors of the essays present a variety of methods, ranging from behavior rating to assessment centers. The authors also show uses of performance assessment in business, medicine, law, teaching, and evaluation of communications skills.

Boyer, C. M., Ewell, P. T., Finney, J. E., and Mingle, J. R. "Assessment and Outcomes Measurement: A View from the States." *AAHE Bulletin,* 1987, *39* (7), 8–12.

These authors report the results of a survey conducted by the Education Commission of the States. The purpose of the survey was to identify trends in state-promoted assessment. Results showed that approximately two-thirds of the states have established or are establishing programs that provide incentives for assessment efforts.

Educational Testing Service. *Assessing the Outcomes of Higher Education: Proceedings of the 1986 ETS Invitational Conference.* Princeton, N.J.: Educational Testing Service, 1987.

Topics addressed in the papers presented at this invitational conference on assessment include the responses of accrediting associations, state agencies, and colleges and universities to the assessment movement; the use of unobtrusive measures in assessing student outcomes; and the role of value-added analyses in assessing educational outcomes.

El-Khawas, E. "Colleges Reclaim the Assessment Initiative." *Educational Record,* 1987, *68* (2), 54–58.

In this article, the author summarizes the results of a recent survey conducted by the American Council on Education (ACE). The author argues that colleges and universities are taking the lead in promoting the assessment of student educational outcomes. According the ACE survey, colleges and universities are developing campus assessment programs designed to improve campus planning, rather than to satisfy external mandates.

Ewell, P. T. "Assessment: Where Are We?" *Change,* 1987, *19* (1), 23–28.

While Ewell briefly examines efforts of private institutions to assess student outcomes, the primary focus is on the response of public institutions to state mandates. Ewell describes several state-mandated approaches and institutional responses to them, as well as several concerns arising from the trend toward state-mandated assessment.

Gronlund, N. E. *Constructing Achievement Tests.* (3d ed.) Englewood Cliffs, N.J.: Prentice-Hall, 1982.

The author provides a basic introduction to constructing achievement tests. Gronlund discusses all phases of test construction and evaluation, including specification of educational objectives, development of test items, and evaluation of test items. Gronlund also identifies differences in construction and scoring between objective and essay examinations.

Henerson, M. E., Morris, L. L., and Fitz-Gibbon, C. T. *How to Measure Attitudes.* Newbury, Park, Calif.: Sage, 1983.

These authors describe a variety of approaches for measuring attitudes, including surveys, interviews, and observations of behavior. They also discuss development, reliability, and validity of instruments.

Marchese, T. J. "Third Down, Ten Years to Go." *AAHE Bulletin,* 1987, *40* (4), 3–8.

Marchese traces the assessment movement over the last three years. The author describes six approaches to assessing educational outcomes:

the assessment center, assessment as learning, assessment as program monitoring, assessment of student development, assessment as standardized testing, and assessing through a senior examiner.

Representative Assessment Programs

The growing interest in educational outcomes has produced a variety of approaches to assessment. The following organizations engage in ongoing assessment. This list represents only a sampling of current programs, but it covers the variety of approaches being used at this time.

Alverno College
Judeen Schute, Alverno College, 3401 South 39th Street, Milwaukee, WI 53215; (414)382-6000. Designs and implements general educational outcomes assessment.

American Association for Higher Education
Patricia Hutchings, American Association for Higher Education, One Dupont Circle NW, Suite 600, Washington, DC 20036; (202)293-6440. Convenes annual forum, supports descriptive studies of assessment, and provides referral service.

Association of American Colleges
Carol Schneider, Association of American Colleges, 1818 R Street NW, Washington, DC 20009; (202)387-3860. Coordinates assessment programs that rely on visiting examiners.

City University of New York, Research Foundation
Harvey S. Wiener, Professor of English, CUNY/Research Foundation, 309 Clearview Lane, Massapequa, NY 11758; (516)799-1951. Assessment of word processing and writing effectiveness.

Educational Testing Service
Roy Hardy, Director, Educational Testing Service, 250 Piedmont Avenue NE, Suite 1240, Atlanta, GA 30308; (404)524-4501. Develops item banks for assessment of learning outcomes in five disciplines.

Harvard Medical School
Gordon Moore, Director, New Pathway Project, Harvard Medical School, 25 Shattuck Street, Boston, MA 02115; (617)732-0634. Conducts comparative assessments of traditional and medical school curriculum models.

Harvard University
Richard Light, Professor, School of Education, Harvard University, Cambridge, MA 02138; (617)495-1183. Manages cooperative pilot project involving assessment at selective institutions.

Indiana University of Pennsylvania
Robert Millward, Director, Pre-Teacher Assessment Center, Indiana University of Pennsylvania, 136 Stouffer Hall, Indiana, PA 15705; (412)357-2480. Establishes pre-teacher assessment in new center that evaluates teaching abilities using classroom simulations.

James Madison University
Dary Erwin, Office of Student Assessment, James Madison University, Harrisonburg, VA 22801; (703)568-6211. Conducts assessment in seven broad areas: major, general education, interdisciplinary objectives, affective development, functional skills, alumni, and environment.

Kean College
Michael Knight, Donald Lumsden, Assessment of Student Learning and Development, Kean College of New Jersey, Union, NJ 07083; (201)527-2000. Uses faculty-developed outcomes assessment in each program area.

King's College
D. W. Farmer, Vice-President and Dean of Academic Affairs, King's College, Wilkes-Barre, PA 18711; (717)826-5900. Uses outcomes-oriented curriculum, complemented by course-embedded assessment program; emphasis on "transferable skills of liberal learning" linked with progress in major.

Miami University of Ohio
Karl Schilling, Associate Dean, Western College Program, Miami University, Oxford, OH 45056; (513)529-1809. Employs comparative assessment of discipline-based and interdisciplinary undergraduate curricula at Miami University of Ohio.

Northeast Missouri State University
Charles J. McClain, President; Darrell Krueger, Dean of Instruction; Administration/Humanities Building, Northeast Missouri State University, Kirskville, MO 63501; (816)785-4100. Employs value-added approach using standardized tests and uses surveys to assess student growth and evaluate the university.

Ohio Board of Regents
Elaine H. Hairston, Vice-Chancellor, Academic and Special Programs, Ohio Board of Regents, 30E Broad Street, 36th Floor, Columbus, OH 43266; (614)466-6000. Promotes excellence, stimulates assessment, and communicates program and institutional improvements to external agencies, on the basis of a statewide assessment project.

Rhode Island College

William Enteman, Provost and Vice-President for Academic Affairs, Rhode Island College, Providence, RI 02908; (401)456-8003. Develops assessment activities linked to curriculum revisions, new advising systems, and individualized educational plans.

South Dakota State University

Kris Smith, Assessment and Testing Office, South Dakota State University, Administration Building, Room 215, Brookings, SD 57007; (605)688-4217. Reviews general educational outcome assessment instruments after trial use; also uses a variety of subject area tests and surveys.

Southern Association of Colleges and Schools

Carol A. Luthman, Assistant Executive Director, Commission on Colleges, Southern Association of Colleges and Schools, 795 Peachtree Street NE, Atlanta, GA 30365; (404)847-6120. Develops manuals describing college use of outcomes assessment during the accreditation process.

State University of New York, Plattsburg

Thomas Moran, Assistant Vice-President for Academic Affairs, SUNY/Plattsburg, Plattsburg, NY 12901; (518)564-2080. Develops new assessment procedures as alternatives to nationally standardized tests.

Texas College and University System

Mary Griffith, Project Director, Community College and Technical Institute Division, Coordinating Board of the Texas College and University System, P.O. Box 12788, Houston, TX 78711; (512)475-0718. Defines college-level skills in reading, writing, and mathematics for subsequent adoption by Texas postsecondary system.

University of Kentucky

Charles Elton, Karen Carey, College of Education, University of Kentucky, 111 Dickey Hall, Lexington, KY 40506; (606)257-2627. Studies value-added approaches to assessing institutional effectiveness.

University of Massachusetts

José P. Mestre, Department of Physics and Astronomy, University of Massachusetts, Amherst, MA 01003; (413)545-2040. Researches and develops computer-assisted problem-solving skills (bilingual: English and Spanish).

University of New Mexico

Scott Obenshain, School of Medicine, University of New Mexico, P.O. Box 508, Albuquerque, NM 87131; (505)277-4823. Currently developing a self-assessment center for medical students.

University of Tennessee, Knoxville

Trudy W. Banta, Gary R. Pike, The Assessment Resource Center, University of Tennessee, 2046 Terrace Avenue, Knoxville, TN 37996-3504; (615)974-0883. Conducts a comprehensive assessment program involving testing in the major and in general education, and surveying students and alumni. Results are used in program reviews and institutional planning and improvement. Conducts workshops and disseminates information about assessment to other colleges and universities.

Gary R. Pike is associate director of the Assessment Resource Center at the University of Tennessee, Knoxville.

Index

A

Abrahamson, M. A. 75, 78
Accreditation, and performance funding, 82, 83, 86
ACT COMP, 22, 82, 83, 90, 92
Adelman, C. P., 99
Alchian, A. A., 70, 78
Alkin, M. C., 70, 74, 76, 78
Alverno College: assessment of learning at, 30, 36, 37, 38, 95, 102; inapplicable model at, 10; noncognitive measures at, 47
American Association for Higher Education (AAHE), 6, 10, 102
American Association for State Colleges and Universities, 10
American Council on Education (ACE), 101
Amidon, E. J., 47, 49
Anderson, J. F., 43, 50
Armstrong, J. R., 100
Armstrong, R. L., 74, 78
Assessment, outcomes: activities in implementing, 15; administrative consistency for, 27; background on, 15-16; beginning, 18; change strategies for, 5-14; changing roles in, 7-8; cognitive measures in, 29-39; complicating factors of, 6-7; concept of, 1-2; consequences unknown for, 17, 18, 19; coordinating, 18-19; costs of, 69-80; and current practice, 19-20; and curriculum review, 25-26; enhancing, 97-98; and expectations exercises, 22-23; focus for, 23; information from, and change, 26-27; initiating, 16-20; interest in, 1-2; interpretation of, 20-23; motives unclear for, 16-17, 18, 19; and negative evidence, 22; noncognitive measures for, 41-52; objective of, 95; organizational issues in implementing, 15-28; perils of, 96; pilot projects for, 19; and planning and budgeting decisions, 24-25; and program reviews, 25; programs of, 102-105; promise of, 76-77, 95-96; rationale for, 69-70; sources on, 99-102; for state performance funding, 81-94; utilization of, 23-26; of value added, 53-67; visibility lacking for, 17-18
Association of American Colleges, 54, 65, 102
Astin, A. W., 8, 13, 26, 27, 99-100

B

Bacon, F., 13
Banta, T. W., 3, 4, 24, 25, 27, 58, 65, 81, 94, 95, 98, 100, 105
Bard, L. L., 42-43, 50
Barnett, H. G., 8, 13
Bean, J., 60, 65
Behavioral Events Analysis, 44
Berdie, D. R., 43, 50
Bereiter, C., 57, 58, 65-66
Bergquist, W. H., 100
Berk, R. A., 42, 45, 48, 50, 100
Bess, J. L., 45, 50
Bethany College (West Virginia), writing samples at, 20
Blake, R., 9, 13
Bok, D., 54, 66
Bowen, H. R., 54, 66, 70, 72, 74, 75, 78
Boyd, H. W., 46, 50
Boyer, C. M., 1, 4, 7, 13, 16, 27, 100
Boyer, E. L., 1, 4
Bradburn, N. M., 43, 51
Bradley, R., 60, 65
Brown, R. D., 49, 50
Bryk, A. S., 60, 66, 67
Buros, O. K., 45
Burstein, L., 63, 66

C

California Polytechnic State University, and general education reform, 26